THE

CATECHUMENATE

AND

THE LAW

Font and Table Series

The Font and Table Series offers pastoral perspectives on Christian baptism, confirmation and eucharist.

Other titles in the series are:

A Catechumenate Needs Everybody: Study Guide for Parish Ministers

At That Time: Cycles and Seasons in the Life of a Christian

Baptism Is a Beginning

Celebrating the Rites of Adult Initiation: Pastoral Reflections

The Church Speaks about Sacraments with Children:
Baptism, Confirmation, Eucharist, Penance

Confirmation: A Parish Celebration

Confirmed as Children, Affirmed as Teens

Finding and Forming Sponsors and Godparents

Guide for Sponsors

How Does a Person Become a Catholic?

How to Form a Catechumenate Team

Infant Baptism: A Parish Celebration

Issues in the Christian Initiation of Children

Readings in the Christian Initiation of Children

Welcoming the New Catholic

When Should We Confirm? The Order of Initiation

Related and available through Liturgy Training Publications:

The Rite of Christian Initiation of Adults (ritual and study editions)

Rito de la Iniciación de Adultos (ritual and study editions)

Catechumenate: A Journal of Christian Initiation

Baptism Sourcebook

Forum Essays series

THE
CATECHUMENATE
AND
THE LAW

A PASTORAL AND CANONICAL

COMMENTARY FOR THE CHURCH IN

THE UNITED STATES

JOHN M. HUELS

Liturgy Training Publications

ACKNOWLEDGMENTS

All translations of canons from the Code of Canon Law are taken from *Code of Canon Law: Latin-English Edition*, ©1983, Canon Law Society of America. Reprinted with permission. All rights reserved.

All translations of documents from the Second Vatican Council are taken from *Documents on the Liturgy 1963 - 1979: Conciliar, Papal, and Curial Texts* (Collegeville: The Liturgical Press, 1982), ©1982, International Committee on English in the Liturgy, Inc. (ICEL). All references to the *Rite of Christian Initiation of Adults* are based on the text and paragraph numbers of the 1988 edition for the United States of America; ©1985, ICEL; ©1988, United States Catholic Conference (USCC). Excerpts from "National Statutes for the Catechumenate," ©1988, USCC. All rights reserved.

Editor: Victoria M. Tufano
Production editor: Deborah Bogaert
Designer and typesetter: Jennifer Carney
This book was typeset in Weiss and printed by BookCrafters.

Copyright ©1994, Archdiocese of Chicago: Liturgy Training Publications, 1800 North Hermitage Avenue, Chicago IL 60622-1101; 1-800-933-1800, FAX 1-800-933-7094. All rights reserved.

Printed in the United States of America

Library of Congress Cataloging–in–Publication Data

Huels, John M.
        The catechumenate and the law: a pastoral and canonical commentary for the Church in the United States / John M. Huels.
                p. cm.–(Font and table series)
Includes bibliographical references and index.
ISBN 1-56854-082-5: $6.95
        1. Catechumens–United States 2. Catechumens (Canon law)
3. Catholic Church–United States–Membership. I. Title.
II Series.
BX935.H84 1994
262.9'4—dc20   94-24026
                                                                              CIP

TABLE of CONTENTS

INTRODUCTION

The final translation of the *Rite of Christian Initiation of Adults* (RCIA) was approved by the National Conference of Catholic Bishops of the United States (NCCB) in 1986, and it became effective on September 1, 1988. As of this date, this is the only ritual of adult initiation that may licitly be used in the Latin rite in the territories of the United States episcopal conference. The new ritual has retained, in a revised and renumbered format, the universal law on the Christian initiation of adults contained in the *editio typica* (typical edition) of 1972. It also interweaves a number of American adaptations and adds "National Statutes for the Catechumenate" (in appendix 3 of the rite), which are binding only in the territories of the United States episcopal conference. The latter adaptations and statutes are each sources of *particular* law. They have the force of law for all dioceses in the United States of America, superseding any other contrary laws, including universal laws that may be contrary to them.

The authority of national bishops' conferences over the liturgy, specifically regarding translations and adaptations of the liturgical books, is given in canon 838, §3 of the *Code of Canon Law*. The general legislative competence of episcopal conferences is defined in canon 455. Conferences can issue general decrees in those cases in which the universal law prescribes it, or by special mandate of the Apostolic See. When a decree has passed in plenary session of the conference by at least a two-thirds majority of the members who have deliberative vote, and after it has been reviewed (*recognitum*) by the Apostolic See, it can be promulgated by the bishops' conference. The decree then goes into effect on the date determined by the conference.

The American bishops enacted the "National Statutes for the Catechumenate" by authorization of the law itself (cf. the *editio typica* of the RCIA, *Rituale Romanum, Ordo Initiationis Christianae Adultorum* [Typis Polyglottis Vaticanis, 1972], 20 [the content of this paragraph is contained in RCIA, 76 and 77]; canon 788, §3). Likewise, the universal law found in the RCIA allows the national bishops' conferences to make local adaptations in various matters pertaining to adult initiation (cf. especially RCIA, 32–33). Having exercised its power in virtue of universal law, having attained the favorable review of the Apostolic See, and having promulgated and established an effective date of binding force, the National Conference of Catholics Bishops has duly established the final and mandatory version of the RCIA for the United States with its own adaptations and statutes.

The adaptations and statutes of the RCIA enacted by the NCCB supersede any contrary laws whether they be diocesan or other particular laws, or even if they are universal laws. For example, the NCCB decreed that the anointing with the oil of catechumens is reserved for use in the period of the catechumenate and in the period of purification and enlightenment and is not to be included in the preparation rites on Holy Saturday or in the celebration of initiation at the Easter Vigil or at another time (cf. RCIA, 33, §7; NCCB Statutes, 16). Although the universal law in the *editio typica* of the RCIA allows these other options, they are prohibited in the territories of the United States episcopal conference. Even if a new universal law would come into force that again would allow these other options, this new law would not affect the adaptations of the NCCB because particular laws are in no way derogated from (changed) by a universal law unless the universal law would expressly state this (cf. canon 20). Nor could a diocesan bishop validly enact a diocesan law contrary to the NCCB law, because the laws of the episcopal conference, which are approved by the Apostolic See, are from higher authority than are diocesan laws (cf. canon 135, §2).

The *Rite of Christian Initiation of Adults* is a major source of canon law. All of its introductory norms (*praenotanda*), both the general introduction and the introductions to the various sections, as well the many rubrics and the "National Statutes for the Catechumenate," are true ecclesiastical laws with the same binding force as the canons of the *Code of Canon Law* and other ecclesiastical laws. Their interpretation is governed by the principles for interpreting canon law in general (cf. canons 7–22). In addition to the great number of laws in the RCIA itself, there are other sources of canon law, principally the *Code of Canon Law* and other liturgical books, that also have direct consequences for the catechumenate, the sacraments of initiation, the reception of baptized Christians into the full communion of the Catholic church and other aspects of Christian initiation.

Drawing on these various sources of canon law related to Christian initiation, this book treats select canonical issues and pastoral questions that have canonical implications. Among these are the rights and obligations of catechumens and of candidates for reception into full communion; doubts about the validity of baptism or confirmation; the initiation of younger children at celebrations of adult initiation; delay of confirmation; record-keeping; marriage cases; ministers; godparents and sponsors. Certain topics are deliberately omitted from the book; for example, the time and place for celebrating adult initiation. The reason for excluding additional topics is because the laws governing them are readily located in one place and/or they are self-explanatory and do not need further commentary.

1
CATECHUMENS

Acatechumen is a person who, with the intention of becoming a Christian, undertakes a period of spiritual and catechetical formation in preparation for sacramental initiation into the church. Sometimes the catechumenate is spoken of broadly to include the period of the precatechumenate before the rite of acceptance into the order of catechumens. The term *catechumen* is also used at times in a strict sense to exclude the *elect*, those who have enrolled their names at the beginning of the second step in Christian initiation (RCIA, 118). The NCCB statutes specify the juridical meaning of *catechumen* as "the unbaptized who have been admitted into the order of catechumens" (no. 2), which includes the period of purification and enlightenment. The rights and obligations of a catechumen, therefore, pertain to individuals from the time of their acceptance into the order of catechumens until their reception of baptism. The *inquirers* who show interest in the faith before their formal admission into the catechumenate cannot be afforded the rights that canon law grants to catechumens. In places where the formal catechumenate has not yet been established, a catechumen can be considered to be any unbaptized person who has expressed to the parish priest or other responsible representative of the church his or her intention to be baptized, and has been accepted by the pastor or other minister for preparation for the sacraments of initiation.

Catechumens have a special place in canon law. They are not yet members of the faithful (*christifideles*), that is, those who are baptized, but they have a unique status due to their intention to receive baptism. Canon 206 of the *Code of Canon Law* addresses the fundamental relationship between the catechumen and the church.

> §1. Catechumens are in union with the church in a special manner, that is, under the influence of the Holy Spirit, they ask to be incorporated in the church by explicit choice and are therefore united with the church by that choice just as by a life of faith, hope and charity which they lead; the church already cherishes them as its own.

> §2. The church has special care for catechumens; the church invites them to lead the evangelical life and introduces them to the celebration of sacred rites, and grants them various prerogatives which are proper to Christians.

The canon is based principally on *Lumen gentium*, 14, and *Ad gentes*, 14, of Vatican II. The latter document, the "Decree on the Church's Missionary Activity," states that catechumens "are already joined to the church, already part of Christ's household." The former document, the "Dogmatic Constitution on the Church," says that Mother Church already embraces catechumens as her own. But how is it possible for catechumens already to be joined to the church, to be part of Christ's household, when baptism is required for membership in the church? (cf. canons 96, 204, 205 and 849)

The reference to the "household" of Christ is found in St. Augustine.[1] In the fourth and fifth centuries, catechumens were regarded not as pagans but as Christians, even though they did not yet belong to the faithful.[2] It was common at the time to postpone baptism until later in life, even in the case of those who came from Christian families. Doubtless this was due in part to the rigorous penitential discipline of the day, which could be avoided by sinners who were not baptized. Because the catechumens already believed in the name of Christ, Augustine said, they belonged to Christ's household and could be saved. Although unbaptized and not capable of receiving the sacraments, they were treated in many respects more as Christians than as pagans.

Baptism is necessary for salvation, either by water and the Trinitarian formula, or by intention (canon 849), which is called the "baptism of desire." Although they have not yet been regenerated by the cleansing water of baptism, catechumens, under the influence of the Holy Spirit, desire to receive it. Because they have publicly announced their intention to accept baptism, and because they are attempting to lead a life of faith, hope and charity, they enjoy a special juridical status in the church, called the order of catechumens, which entitles them to certain prerogatives enjoyed by Christians.

MARRIAGE IN THE CHURCH

Marriages in the Catholic church are generally celebrated only when at least one party is Catholic (cf. canons 1109–1110). Among the privileges of being a catechumen, however, is the right to celebrate one's marriage in the church. This right extends to two catechumens who wish to marry and to a catechumen who wishes to marry an unbaptized person who is not a catechumen (RCIA, 47). It also includes a catechumen who wishes to marry a baptized, non-Catholic person (NCCB Statutes, 10). The canonical issues surrounding the marriage of catechumens are discussed in chapter nine of this book.

RIGHT TO A CATHOLIC FUNERAL

Another privilege of catechumens, also found in the former law (1917 *Code of Canon Law*, canon 1239, §2), is the right to Christian burial (RCIA, 47; NCCB Statutes, 8), that is, the right to have one's funeral rites celebrated in the Catholic church. In respect to funerals, catechumens are equated with Catholics (canon 1183, §1). Unlike the case of unbaptized children whose parents intended to have them baptized (canon 1183, §2), no permission is needed for a catechumen's funeral to be celebrated by the Catholic minister using the *Order of Christian Funerals*.

The funeral rites ordinarily are celebrated in three stages: the vigil service at the funeral home or at another place, the funeral Mass in the church and the service at the place of burial or cremation. Catechumens have a right to all three services, just as Catholics do, in places where the three-station liturgy is observed. In the celebration of the funeral rites, the minister should take care to omit language referring to baptism and the other sacraments, which the catechumen was not yet able to receive. The funeral Mass may be omitted at the discretion of the pastor in view of the sensibilities of the immediate family of the deceased catechumen (NCCB Statutes, 9). The pastor or other minister should consult the next of kin or other family representative who is making the funeral arrangements to determine whether the funeral Mass is desired.

The parish responsible for the deceased catechumen's funeral rites is the parish in which the catechumen resided either by way of domicile or quasi-domicile (cf. canons 1177, §1, and 102). The catechumen or those commissioned to arrange for his or her funeral also have a right to choose another church for the funeral with the consent of the pastor or rector of that church; the proper pastor of the departed catechumen should be notified if another church is chosen (canon 1177, §2).

SACRAMENTALS AND SUFFRAGES

The 1917 *Code of Canon Law* permitted blessings to be given to catechumens (canon 1149), a provision also found in the revised code (canon 1170). This pertains not only to the blessings found in the section of the RCIA pertaining to the period of the catechumenate, but to all blessings of the church whether public or private. Already in the year 1919 the Holy See declared that other sacramentals publicly administered were included in the interpretation of this canon such that catechumens may be admitted to the imposition of ashes and the giving of candles and palms.[3] Now the liturgical law says explicitly that catechumens may "receive blessings and other sacramentals" (RCIA, 47).

The NCCB Statutes state that catechumens should be encouraged to seek blessings and other suffrages from the church (no. 8). Among these suffrages are the optional exorcisms found in the RCIA. The blessings and exorcisms of the RCIA can even be given to those who, strictly speaking, are not catechumens, namely, the inquirers during the period of the precatechumenate (RCIA, 40). The rite says that "during the precatechumenate period, parish priests (pastors) should help those taking part in it with prayers suited to them, for example, by celebrating for their spiritual well-being the prayers of exorcism and the blessings given in the ritual" (nn. 94 and 97). This norm is not an exception to the law, because even non-Catholics may receive blessings unless a church prohibition precludes it (canon 1170). The minister of the blessings and minor exorcisms of the catechumens (or inquirers) is a priest or deacon, or a qualified catechist appointed by the bishop for this ministry (RCIA, 91, 96 and 16). Exorcisms that are not minor exorcisms are celebrated only by a priest or deacon (RCIA, 144). The ministers of other blessings are defined in the various liturgical books, principally in the *Book of Blessings*.

Another sacramental that may be administered to catechumens is the anointing with the oil of catechumens. This anointing is optional; it may be celebrated whenever it seems beneficial or desirable during the period of the catechumenate (RCIA, 98), but not on Holy Saturday or immediately before baptism (RCIA, 33, §7; NCCB Statutes, 16). The presiding celebrant of the anointing is a priest or deacon (RCIA, 98). He should use the oil of catechumens blessed by the bishop at the most recent Chrism Mass, but for pastoral reasons a priest (not a deacon) may bless oil for the rite immediately before the anointing (cf. RCIA, 101; *Rite of the Blessing of Oils, Rite of Consecrating the Chrism*, Introduction, 7). Examples of pastoral reasons for a priest to bless the oil would include the unavailability of oil blessed by the bishop or, even when oil blessed by the bishop is available, the desire to bring out more fully the symbolic meaning of the anointing. This blessing by the priest will help fulfill the admonition of n. 99 of the RCIA:

> Care is to be taken that the catechumens understand the significance of the anointing with oil. The anointing with oil symbolizes their need for God's help and strength so that, undeterred by the bonds of the past and overcoming the opposition of the devil, they will forthrightly take the step of professing their faith and will hold fast to it unfalteringly throughout their lives.

Olive oil traditionally is preferred, but the law permits the use of oil that is made from other plants (cf. canon 847, §1). The celebrant anoints the catechumen on the breast or on both hands or, if it seems desirable, even on other parts of the body (RCIA, 105).

Catechumens also are encouraged to take part in celebrations of the word of God. The RCIA mentions three such celebrations: first, celebrations held especially for the catechumens; second, the liturgy of the word at Sunday Mass; third, celebrations held in connection with catechetical instruction (RCIA, 81).

OBLIGATIONS OF CATECHUMENS

It may be misleading to speak of the canonical obligations of catechumens because ecclesiastical law binds only Catholics who have sufficient use of reason and are at least seven years of age (canon 11). Because catechumens are not yet Catholic, they are not obliged to observe ecclesiastical laws. They are, however, bound to the divine law and, consequently, to whatever in canon law is of the divine law. For example, in the law of marriage they are bound by the impediment of prior bond (canon 1085); they would not be free to marry if they or their intended spouse were previously married and the former spouse were still living. In such a case an annulment or dissolution of the previous marriage would be necessary in order for the church to recognize the subsequent marriage as valid.

Although catechumens are not generally bound to observe merely ecclesiastical laws, there are obligations in canon law that indirectly or implicitly bind them. These are the obligations that flow from their responsibilities as catechumens. Catechumens willingly undertake the demands of the catechumenate—such as religious instruction, spiritual formation and apostolic activity—in order to be prepared and found ready for sacramental initiation into the church. They freely choose to take on these obligations; the obligations are self-imposed, even though the precise nature of these obligations comes from an extrinsic source, the church. Nevertheless, they are

truly obligatory, because if these requirements are not sufficiently fulfilled by the catechumen, he or she will not be found
worthy by the church's pastors of being admitted to the order
of the faithful.

The duties of catechumens that are contained in the *Code
of Canon Law* and the liturgical law of the RCIA more often consist of general moral and spiritual exhortations than of specific disciplinary directives. For example, the foundational canon
on catechumens in the code, canon 206, already quoted,
speaks in general, descriptive terms of the responsibilities of
catechumens without using the language of obligation. It says
that catechumens lead "a life of faith, hope and charity" and
that "the church invites them to lead the evangelical life and
introduces them to the celebration of the sacred rites." By
implication, if catechumens are not attempting to lead an
evangelical life of faith, hope and charity or are not sufficiently partaking in the sacred rites of the church warranted by
their status and circumstances, then they will not be fulfilling
their obligations as catechumens and likely would not be
judged ready for sacramental initiation.

Other principal obligations in canon law that bind catechumens include:

1. assuming an apprenticeship in the Christian life and suitable
   initiation into the mystery of salvation and the life of faith
   (canon 788, §2)

2. accepting a formation leading to a thorough understanding of
   the gospel truth and baptismal duties, and to a love of Christ
   and his church (canon 789)

3. participating in the stages of initiation to the extent possible,
   including appropriate liturgical rites during the proper seasons
   (canon 851; RCIA, 6, 8)

4. undertaking sufficient instruction in the truths of the faith and
   in Christian duties, including an appropriate acquaintance with
   dogmas and precepts; contrition for personal sins; and evi-
   dence of faith, conversion and of entering a relationship with
   God in Christ (canon 865, §1; RCIA, 42; 75, §1; 120; 139; 142)

5. learning to turn more readily to God in prayer, to bear witness to the faith, to keep their hopes set on Christ in all things, to follow supernatural inspiration in their deeds, and to practice love of neighbor, even at the cost of self-renunciation (RCIA, 75, §2)

6. learning how to work actively with others to spread the gospel and to build up the church by the witness of their lives and by professing their faith, thus manifesting by social consequences a progressive change of outlook and conduct (RCIA, 75, §§2 and 4)

7. seeking blessings, sacramentals and other suffrages of the church so that they may receive courage, joy and peace as they proceed along their difficult journey; partaking in celebrations of the word of God; learning to keep holy the Lord's Day by participating in the liturgy of the word on Sundays (NCCB Statutes, 8; RCIA, 47; 75, §1; 83; 95)

8. at the appropriate time, memorizing the Creed and reciting it publicly (RCIA, 148, 193–196)

9. choosing godparents on the basis of their example, good qualities and friendship and on the basis of the other requirements of canon law (RCIA, 11, 80, 123; canon 874)

10. on Holy Saturday before their initiation, refraining from their usual activities, spending their time in prayer and reflection and, so far as they can, observing a fast (RCIA, 185, §1; NCCB Statutes, 15); and immediately before their baptism, renouncing their sins and making a profession of faith (RCIA, 211, 223–225).

Although catechumens generally are not bound to canon law, there are certain expectations of them enunciated in the code and the liturgical law. These duties are fashioned largely as generalized exhortations rather than as specific obligations, but they are not lacking in juridical consequences. If these expectations are not sufficiently fulfilled by a catechumen, he or she will not be deemed worthy of advancement in the steps of initiation and ultimately will be excluded from the order of the faithful.

It is the responsibility of the bishop, priests, deacons,

catechists, godparents and the entire community, especially those involved in the catechumenate, to see that these obligations are fulfilled by catechumens during the course of their preparation for sacramental initiation. The major judgment on a catechumen's suitability is made by the community and its leaders, in accord with their respective responsibilities, before admission to the rite of election (RCIA, 121).

ENDNOTES

1. *Tractatus in Joannis Evangelium*, XI, 4; *Patrologiae Latinae* (PL) 35: 1476; see also RCIA, 47.

2. Augustine, ibid., XLIV, 2; PL 35:1714.

3. Congregation of Rites, reply, March 8, 1919, *Acta Apostolicae Sedis* (AAS) 11 (1919), 144.

2
CANDIDATES FOR RECEPTION INTO FULL COMMUNION

Candidates for reception into the full communion of the Catholic church are already baptized; therefore, they are not catechumens. They already belong to the order of the faithful by virtue of their baptism, as is clear from canon 204, §1, of the code:

> The Christian faithful are those who, inasmuch as they have been incorporated in Christ through baptism, have been constituted as the people of God; for this reason, since they have become sharers in Christ's priestly, prophetic and royal office in their own manner, they are called to exercise the mission which God has entrusted to the church to fulfill in the world, in accord with the condition proper to each one.

Candidates for reception into full communion should, insofar as possible, be given a separate formation from those who are candidates for baptism, and they should not undergo the various stages and rites proper to the catechumenate (cf. NCCB Statutes, 30–31). Whenever catechumens and candidates for reception into full communion appear together in liturgical ceremonies, such as at celebrations of the word, the distinction between the two classes of persons should be obvious to all, and ecumenical sensitivities should be respected (cf. NCCB Statutes, 31, 34). The general principle stated in RCIA, 477, should always be kept in mind: "Anything that would equate candidates for reception with those who are catechumens is to be absolutely avoided."

Reception into full communion should take place at the Sunday eucharist in the parish community, but not ordinarily at the Easter Vigil, in order to avoid any confusion of baptized

Christians with candidates for baptism and to avoid triumphalism in the liturgical welcome into the Catholic eucharistic community (NCCB Statutes, 33). Although it is not preferred, it is nevertheless permissible for baptized non-Catholics to be received into full communion at the Easter Vigil when the catechumens are initiated, observing part III, chapter four, of the RCIA, "Celebration at the Easter Vigil of the Sacraments of Initiation and the Rite of Reception into Full Communion of the Catholic Church" (RCIA, 562–594; NCCB Statutes, 34).

RIGHTS OF BAPTIZED NON-CATHOLICS

Baptized non-Catholics belong to the church of Christ and are linked in a real, though imperfect, communion to the Catholic faithful (Vatican II, "Decree on Ecumenism," 3; *Directory for Ecumenism* [DE], 129). Because they are not in full communion, non-Catholic Christians do not enjoy all the rights of Catholics (cf. canons 96, 205). Canon law does, however, give certain rights and privileges to separated Christians in general, and a few that are specific to baptized persons preparing for reception into full communion. Among these are:

1. sharing in worship in conformity with the provisions of the *Ecumenical Directory* and the *Code of Canon Law* (RCIA, 477; canon 844)

2. being a witness at a Catholic baptism (canon 874, §2), or, in the case of separated Eastern Christians, being a godparent at a Catholic baptism (DE, 98b)

3. receiving blessings and other sacramentals, except in a case where a prohibition precludes this (canon 1170)

4. having their funeral rites celebrated in the Catholic church, in the prudent judgment of the local ordinary, provided it is not evidently contrary to the wishes of the non-Catholic departed person and provided his or her own minister is unavailable (canon 1183, §3)

5. participating in liturgical rites marking their progress in formation, as included in part II, chapter four, of the RCIA,

"Preparation of Uncatechized Adults for Confirmation and Eucharist" (RCIA, 478; NCCB Statutes, 31)

6. participation in celebrations of the word, including those intended for catechumens (NCCB Statutes, 31).

In the early church, catechumens were dismissed after the liturgy of the word because the sacraments, the sacred "mysteries," were a carefully guarded secret open only to the initiated. Unlike catechumens, candidates for reception into full communion are already baptized and thus are capable of participating, to the extent allowed by law, in the sacraments of the church. Although they may not yet, as a rule, receive holy communion, the candidates' presence at the entire eucharistic celebration is a clear way of signifying that they already are members of the faithful, though they are not yet in full communion. Their presence at the liturgy of the eucharist would be a strong affirmation of the dignity of their baptism in their original church, and a clear sign to them, to the catechumens, and to the entire community that baptism does indeed make a difference.

While the ideal practice is for candidates to remain for the entire eucharist, they are not obliged to remain because the precept to attend Mass on Sundays and holy days binds only Catholics (canon 1247), including those Catholics seven and older who have not yet been catechized. In some places there are few catechumens and candidates, so it is not possible to provide a separate formation for each of them.

If it is necessary that both candidates and catechumens leave the Sunday assembly after the liturgy of the word, there should be some ritual indication acknowledging their different status. For example, the candidates and catechumens could sit on separate sides of the church, and the presider could invite each group to rise separately and then dismiss each group successively. Using the first dismissal rite, the presider would say: "Catechumens, go in peace, and may the Lord remain with you always" (RCIA, 67 A). He would then address the candidates with similar words. Another option, albeit the least preferred, would be to have no dismissal and have both catechumens and candidates remain for the entire eucharist (RCIA, 67 C).

OBLIGATIONS OF CANDIDATES FOR RECEPTION INTO FULL COMMUNION

Because candidates for reception into full communion are not yet Catholic, they are not bound to observe ecclesiastical laws (canon 11) but are bound to the divine law. Like catechumens, they also must observe what is required of them in preparation for reception into full communion, namely:

1. accepting doctrinal and spiritual preparation, adapted to individual pastoral requirements depending on the extent to which the baptized person has led a Christian life within a community of faith (RCIA, 477; NCCB Statutes, 30)

2. pursuing appropriate catechesis in order to deepen an inner adherence to the church where the fullness of one's baptism is found (RCIA, 477; NCCB Statutes, 30)

3. participating in the sacrament of reconciliation prior to, but distinct from, the reception into full communion when it takes place within Mass, informing the confessor that he or she is about to be received into full communion (RCIA, 482; NCCB Statutes, 36)

4. making a profession of faith consisting of the Nicene Creed and the words, "I believe and profess all that the holy Catholic Church believes, teaches, and proclaims to be revealed by God" (RCIA, 491).

In reference to the candidates' celebration of the sacrament of penance before their reception into full communion, RCIA, 482, states in part: "If the profession of faith and reception take place within Mass, the candidate, according to his or her own conscience, should make a confession of sins beforehand, first informing the confessor that he or she is about to be received into full communion." It should be noted that the English translation of the phrase "according to his or her own conscience" could convey the false impression that the sacrament of reconciliation is wholly optional according to the desires of the candidate.

The original Latin (*attenta sua personali condicione*) does not have this optional sense. A literal translation is "having considered his or her own personal condition"; that is, having reflected on his or her own personal history, life circumstances, and especially any serious sins committed after baptism, the candidate should celebrate the sacrament of penance according to the first or second rite of penance, either of which provide for individual confession and absolution.

As for the preceptive nature of the law, the verb used (*confiteatur*) is a jussive subjunctive, commonly translated "should confess" or "is to confess." It is not as strongly preceptive as a command in the indicative mood, but it indicates the practice that normally ought to be observed.[1]

It is important that all baptized candidates be prepared for the sacrament of reconciliation and receive it prior to the celebration of the rite of reception into full communion. According to church doctrine and law, it is necessary that the candidates confess individually all *serious sins* in number and in kind that they recall having committed during their life after they were baptized (canons 960, 989, 916). However, even those who have lived exemplary lives and have committed no serious sins would benefit from the grace of the sacrament, and they would profit from the preparation for and experience of making an individual confession as in the first or second rite of penance. This formative experience provides a solid foundation for their future sacramental lives as Catholic faithful. For this reason the NCCB Statutes, 36, urge that part of the formation of candidates should include catechesis on the frequent celebration of penance.

Baptized persons who are preparing for reception into full communion are generally not given special treatment in canon law. They are juridically equatable to other baptized non-Catholics. Thus, for example, when such a baptized person who intends to become a Catholic marries a Catholic, it is considered a mixed marriage and the necessary permission must be obtained (canon 1124). In this case it also is required of the Catholic party to the marriage to declare that he or she is prepared to remove dangers of falling away from the faith and to make a sincere promise to do all in his or her power to have all the children baptized and brought up in the Catholic church (canon 1125, 1°). In such cases, however, a dispensation from this requirement should be sought from the diocesan bishop because it can be presumed that a person intending to become a Catholic would neither pose a danger to the faith of the Catholic party nor would prevent the children from being baptized and raised Catholic.

ENDNOTES

1. For further discussion on the various literary forms in canon law, see my booklet, *Liturgical Law: An Introduction*, cited in appendix A.

3
INVALID AND DOUBTFUL BAPTISM AND CONFIRMATION

Candidates from religious denominations that do not have valid baptism, even though they consider themselves Christian, are juridically equivalent to catechumens. They are not members of the faithful and so are eligible to undergo the full catechumenal process with all its steps. If they already possess "a depth of Christian conversion and a degree of religious maturity," or if there are other good reasons for their not observing the standard catechumenate, it may be desirable in some cases to seek the permission of the bishop to follow the abbreviated catechumenate of the "Rite of Christian Initiation of Adults in Exceptional Circumstances" (cf., NCCB Statutes, 20; RCIA, 331–339). If the lack or invalidity of baptism is not certain, that is, if there is a doubt whether there may have been a valid baptism, then the candidate is not treated as a catechumen but is given the formation appropriate to baptized non-Catholics who are being prepared for reception into full communion.

THOSE BAPTIZED AND CONFIRMED IN THE SEPARATED EASTERN CHURCHES

The 1993 *Directory for Ecumenism* (DE) states that there can be no doubt about the validity of baptism conferred in the separated Eastern churches (DE, 99a). In the case of a candidate who was baptized in one of these churches and wishes to be received into the Catholic church, it suffices simply to have a baptismal certificate. If a baptismal certificate or other documentary proof of baptism cannot be obtained, the usual way to prove baptism is to obtain the oath of the baptized person, if he or she were baptized as an adult, that is, was seven or older and had the use of reason (canons 852, §1; 876). In the case of a person baptized as an infant, the declaration of a single witness who is above suspicion ordinarily suffices to prove baptism (cf. canon 876).

The Eastern churches also have valid confirmation, which is administered immediately after baptism. Hence, candidates baptized in these churches may not be confirmed in the Catholic church because confirmation, like baptism and holy orders, imparts a character and cannot be repeated (canon 845, §1). Even if the baptismal certificate makes no mention that confirmation has been conferred, there is no reason for doubting that it was; confirmation is routinely administered after baptism in these churches (DE, 99a). When Eastern Christians enter the fullness of Catholic communion, they need only make a profession of faith; the liturgical rite of reception into full communion is not observed (RCIA, 474).

ESTABLISHING THE FACT OR VALIDITY OF BAPTISM

Those being received into full communion from other churches or ecclesial communities are not to be baptized or conditionally baptized unless there is a reasonable doubt whether they were baptized or whether the baptism was validly conferred. Only if the doubt remains after a serious investigation of the relevant facts can the minister proceed to baptize conditionally (canon 869, §1; RCIA, 480; NCCB Statutes, 37). The investigation should include an examination of the matter and the form of words used in the conferral of baptism, and a consideration of the intention of the adult being baptized and of the minister of baptism (canon 869, §2). Indiscriminate conditional baptism of those seeking full communion is forbidden (cf. DE, 95–99).

Baptism with water, whether by immersion, pouring or sprinkling, together with the Trinitarian formula, is of itself valid. Baptism by sprinkling, while not licitly permitted in the Latin church (canon 854), is nevertheless valid provided the water touches the person being baptized. If the rituals, liturgical books or customs of some church or ecclesial community prescribe baptism with water and the Trinitarian formula, one need not doubt that it was performed validly unless there is some reason to suspect that the minister did not observe the regulations of his or her own church or community. To establish proof of valid baptism conferred in a non-Catholic denomination that uses water and the Trinitarian formula, it generally suffices to have a baptismal certificate with the name of the minister on it (DE, 95a).

Sufficient intention on the part of the adult being baptized or on the part of the minister should be presumed. The adult must intend to be baptized in the church of Christ and observe the commandments of the Christian religion (canon 865, §2). Those baptized as infants—children under seven and those who lack sufficient use of reason—are validly baptized without this minimal intention. The minister must have the intention of doing what the church does when it baptizes. Only if there are serious grounds for doubting whether either the adult being baptized or the minister of baptism lacked the requisite intention would it be justified after a serious investigation to baptize conditionally. Insufficient faith on the part of the minister has no effect on the validity of baptism (DE, 95b).

If, after a serious investigation has taken place, a reasonable doubt remains about the fact or validity of baptism, the candidate for reception into full communion can be baptized conditionally. Before conditional baptism, the doctrine of baptism must be explained to the person, if he or she is an adult; the reasons for the doubtful validity of the baptism must also be explained to the adult recipient or to the parents in the case of infant baptism (canon 869, §3). Conditional baptism is conferred privately, not solemnly at a public liturgical assembly of the community. The complete rite of baptism is not used, but only those parts are included as are determined by the diocesan bishop. The reception into full communion takes place following conditional baptism at a later date during the Sunday eucharist of the community (RCIA, 480; NCCB Statutes, 37).

ESTABLISHING the VALIDITY of CONFIRMATION

Confirmation is valid only in those churches that have the valid sacrament of holy orders. Besides the separated Eastern churches, this would include the Old Catholic, Old Roman Catholic and Polish National Churches. The Protestant denominations are not recognized as having valid orders, so persons baptized in those ecclesial communities should be confirmed during the rite of reception into full communion.

4
INITIATING CHILDREN
WITH ADULTS

Two categories of children, or minors, exist in canon law. In the first category are children under seven years of age and those who lack the use of reason; in the second category are those from ages seven through seventeen who have the use of reason (cf. canons 11, 97). An adult is one who is eighteen years or older and has the use of reason (canon 97, §1). There is an exception to this rule in reference to baptism, however, whereby an adult is considered to be anyone seven or older with the use of reason (canon 852, §1). Therefore, those who are under seven years of age, as well as those who lack the use of reason, are baptized according to the *Rite of Baptism for Children*. Those who are seven years or older and have the use of reason are baptized according to the *Rite of Christian Initiation of Adults*. By exception, children below the age of seven who already have attained a sufficient use of reason can also be considered children of catechetical age and can follow the pattern of adult initiation (cf. NCCB Statutes, 18).

The law gives no upper age limit on those who are considered children of catechetical age, but the age of fourteen could be recommended as the standard upper age because it has a certain significance in canon law with reference to baptism. At age fourteen a person is free to choose to be baptized in any ritual church—in the Latin rite or an Eastern rite (canon 111, §2). Parents no longer can choose the rite of their children when they are fourteen or older, even when they themselves transfer to a new rite; and if children under fourteen were transferred to a new rite by their parents, they are free to return to their ritual church of baptism when they reach fourteen years of age (canon 112, §1, 3°). Another significant reference to the age of fourteen occurs in canon 863, which states, "The baptism of adults, at least of those who have completed fourteen years of age, is to be referred to the bishop so that it may be conferred by him, if he judges it expedient."

These references in the law suggest a special significance about the age of fourteen in relation to baptism. It seems appropriate, therefore, that minors who are fourteen and older should ordinarily be received into the church by the process in part I, chapter one, of the *Rite of Christian Initiation of Adults*.

INITIATING CHILDREN

The RCIA contains a chapter devoted to the "Christian Initiation of Children Who Have Reached Catechetical Age" (part II, chapter one, 252–330). According to the RCIA, 252:

> Such children are capable of receiving and nurturing a personal faith and of recognizing an obligation in conscience. But they cannot yet be treated as adults because, at this stage of their lives, they are dependent on their parents or guardians and are still strongly influenced by their companions and their social surroundings.

The procedure outlined in this section is used to its best advantage with a group of several children, because they can help each other by example in their progress as catechumens (RCIA, 255).

INITIATING CHILDREN with THEIR PARENTS

It frequently happens that children, both those who are of catechetical age and younger children, come to Christian initiation together with their parents and other adults; sometimes even their preparation takes place together with adults. In such cases the steps of initiation as defined in part I of the RCIA—the order for adults—is observed, but adaptations in the formation of the candidates and in the ritual celebrations of the various steps can be made to take account more fittingly of the presence and condition of children of various ages.

The NCCB Statutes state:

> Since children who have reached the use of reason are considered, for purposes of Christian initiation, to be adults (canon 852, §1), their formation should follow the general pattern of the ordinary catechumenate as far as possible, with the appropriate adaptations permitted by the ritual. They should receive the sacraments of baptism, confirmation and eucharist at the Easter Vigil, together with the older catechumens. (18)

The general principles to be observed in making adaptations in these cases are found in the *General Introduction to Christian Initiation*, 34–35; in the RCIA, especially nn. 35, 253 and 259; and in the *Rite of Baptism for Children*, 27–31. Special note should be taken of n. 28 of the latter rite, which defines the adaptations necessary when the baptism of children is celebrated as part of the Easter Vigil.

Whenever children are initiated together with adults, chief consideration should be given to the situation of the adults, and that is why the rite in part I, intended for adults, is the basic model that is followed. Suitable accommodations can then be made as appropriate for the situation of children without detracting, however, from the primarily adult character of the rite.

Greater adaptation may be needed when children are below the age of discretion. At the baptism of such children with their parent(s), the renunciation of sin and profession of faith by the parent(s) supplies for the children's profession and so it should not be repeated. However, the questions and admonitions in the *Rite of Baptism for Children*, 38–39, 56 and 60, should be included, if possible. When a number of children below catechetical age are being baptized together with adults, it is important that these questions and admonitions not be prolonged so as to detract from the adult character of the celebration. This can be done by addressing all the parents together and, insofar as possible, having them respond in unison to the questions (cf. *Rite of Baptism for Children*, 38).

5
DELAYING CONFIRMATION

anon 842, §2, of the *Code of Canon Law* says that the "sacraments of baptism, confirmation and the most holy eucharist are so interrelated that they are required for full Christian initiation." The *General Introduction to Christian Initiation*, 1 and 2, also speaks of the close connections among the three sacraments of initiation. The *Rite of Christian Initiation of Adults*, faithful to the practice of the ancient church, calls for the celebration of baptism, confirmation and eucharist together in a single and unified rite of initiation; the three sacraments are interrelated actions within the total initiatory celebration. The law of the National Conference of Catholic Bishops is fully in accord with these provisions of universal law:

> In order to signify clearly the interrelation or coalescence of the three sacraments which are required for full Christian initiation, adult candidates, including children of catechetical age, are to receive baptism, confirmation and eucharist in a single eucharistic celebration, whether at the Easter Vigil or, if necessary, at some other time. (NCCB Statutes, 14)

The celebration of the three sacraments of initiation in the same celebration is normative; it is the way it should be done. The delay of confirmation and/or eucharist after baptism is the exception, even though the exceptions are numerous due to the practice in the Western church of deferring confirmation and first communion after infant baptism until the child attains the age of reason.

It is rare that eucharist is delayed after adult baptism, but the practice of delaying confirmation unfortunately still persists in some places, perhaps as a result of misguided pastoral concerns or uninformed judgments about the nature of confirmation. The *Code of Canon Law*, canon 879, briefly describes the significance of confirmation:

> The sacrament of confirmation impresses a character and by it the baptized, continuing on the path of Christian initiation, are enriched by the gift of the Holy Spirit and bound more perfectly to the church; it strengthens them and obliges them more firmly to be witnesses to Christ by word and deed and to spread and defend the faith.

This canon reveals that confirmation is a continuation and deepening of one's baptismal life and commitments. It is the second sacrament of Christian life, the second principal action in the celebration of Christian initiation. It follows that confirmation typically should precede the reception of first communion, ideally in the same celebration to maintain the interrelatedness of the sacraments of initiation, even when the reception of the latter two sacraments is delayed in the case of infant baptism.

Canon 879 also notes certain effects of confirmation: the gift of the Holy Spirit, a stronger bond to the church, a strengthening of the baptized for the apostolate and the resultant greater duty on the part of the confirmed to be witnesses to Christ and to spread and defend the faith by word and example. The *General Introduction to Christian Initiation*, 2, speaks in similar words of the effects of confirmation:

> By signing us with the gift of the Spirit, confirmation makes us more completely the image of the Lord and fills us with the Holy Spirit, so that we may bear witness to him before all the world and work to bring the Body of Christ to its fullness as soon as possible.

Because confirmation and eucharist are so closely related to baptism, and because they complete Christian initiation, confirmation and first communion should never be delayed, except after infant baptism, unless there is a grave reason (cf. RCIA, 24, 215). Without confirmation and eucharist, Christian initiation is incomplete, and the rite of initiation is truncated.

Likewise, those who are baptized as adults or children of catechetical age without receiving confirmation or eucharist are denied sacraments to which they are entitled by law and also are denied the graces and benefits of the sacraments.

Among the effects of confirmation and eucharist are some that are properly juridical, affecting the status of the faithful. Those who are baptized Catholics but who have not received confirmation and eucharist are not fully initiated into the Catholic church; they are in some respects juridically equivalent to separated Christians from ecclesial communities that lack valid confirmation and eucharist. For example, those who are not fully initiated are not eligible to be godparents (canon 874, §1, 3°). Those who are not confirmed may not licitly receive holy orders (canons 1033; 1050, 3°) or enter the novitiate (canon 645, §1) or the seminary (canon 241, §1). Furthermore, Catholics are required to be confirmed before they marry, if this can be done without serious inconvenience (canon 1065, §1).

Certain fundamental rights and obligations of laypersons emanate from the reception of both baptism and confirmation, notably their deputation for the apostolate, that they might "work as individuals or in associations so that the divine message of salvation becomes known and accepted by persons throughout the world" (canon 225, §1) and that they be "witnesses to the gospel message by word and by example of Christian life" (canon 759). Clearly, initiation into the church is not complete without confirmation and eucharist. Therefore, confirmation and eucharist can be delayed only in the case of infant baptism, or in the case of adult baptism, only for serious reasons. This also applies to children of catechetical age (NCCB Statutes, 14).

Children of catechetical age are considered adults in reference to baptism and are initiated according to the RCIA, part II, chapter one, "Christian Initiation of Children Who Have Reached Catechetical Age." Or, when they are together with adults, they are initiated according to part I of the RCIA, with adaptations made for the presence of children. They are to receive the sacraments of baptism, confirmation and eucharist at the Easter Vigil, together with the older catechumens (RCIA, 305; NCCB Statutes, 18). This ordinarily applies to all who are at least seven years of age and who have attained the use of reason (canons 852, §1; 97, §2). Those without the use of reason who are unable to make the profession of faith themselves are baptized according to the *Rite of Baptism for Children*.

The standard age for the reception of confirmation in the Latin church is about the age of discretion, that is, about seven years of age (canon 891). Even in places where the competent ecclesiastical authority permits confirmation at a later age, this exception to canon law does not apply in the case of children who are baptized when they are seven or older and have the use of reason. They must be confirmed immediately after baptism irrespective of the age that other children in the parish are confirmed.

The RCIA says that children who are candidates for initiation "should, if possible, come to the sacraments of initiation at the time that their baptized companions are to receive confirmation or eucharist" (n. 256). This does not mean that the confirmation of children of catechetical age can be delayed after their baptism until the age that their companions are receiving it. It means, rather, that if there are children being baptized who are about the same age as children who are being confirmed and making first communion, then the confirmation and first communion of the other children ideally should take place at the same ceremony with the children being baptized so that the latter can receive confirmation and first communion together with their companions (cf. RCIA, 308). The NCCB Statutes, 19, further clarifies this point:

> Some elements of the ordinary catechetical instruction of baptized children before their reception of the sacraments of confirmation and eucharist may be appropriately shared with catechumens of catechetical age. Their condition and status as catechumens, however, should not be compromised or confused, nor should they receive the sacraments of initiation in any sequence other than that determined in the ritual of Christian initiation.

There is a firm legal obligation binding the minister to

confirm adults and children of catechetical age who are baptized or received into the church, even though they may be
below the age that children baptized in infancy normally are
confirmed in that locale. Canon 855, §2, states: "A presbyter
who has this faculty [to confirm] must use it for those in whose
favor the faculty was granted." Whenever they baptize an
adult or a child seven or older, or receive such persons into full
communion, presbyters have the faculty to confirm by law
provided they have a pastoral office or a mandate of the diocesan bishop (canon 883, 2°; NCCB Statutes, 12). The law insists
that when priests have this faculty, they must use it, and they
may not be prohibited from using it (cf. RCIA, 13, 35). The
faithful have a fundamental right to the sacraments (canon
213), including confirmation, and canon law prohibits ministers from denying the sacraments to those who are legally
qualified to receive them (canon 843, §1).

In sum, confirmation and first communion may not licitly
be delayed following the baptism of anyone who is seven or
older and has the use of reason. Likewise, confirmation and
first communion cannot licitly be delayed in the case of some-
one baptized in a non-Catholic ecclesial community who is
being received into full communion. In either case the sacraments of confirmation and eucharist must be administered in
the course of the celebration of initiation or reception. The
only exception permitted in the law is a case where there is a
serious reason for delay (cf. RCIA, 24, 215).

An example of a serious reason for delaying confirmation
is a situation in which a person is in danger of death and is baptized by a deacon or layperson (cf. "Rite of Christian Initiation
in Exceptional Circumstances, Abbreviated Form," RCIA,
340–369, to be used by priests and deacons; and "Rite of
Christian Initiation of a Person in Danger of Death," RCIA,
370–399, ordinarily used by catechists and laypersons).
Because only priests can confirm (canon 882), the person can
be confirmed later by any priest whosoever if he or she
remains in danger of death (cf. canon 883, 3°; RCIA, 374, 400).
Another example of a serious reason for delaying confirmation
would be danger of death when a priest baptizes a person but

does not have the sacred chrism with him. The chrism is the essential matter of the sacrament (canon 880, §1) and must be consecrated by a bishop, even if the sacrament is conferred by a presbyter (canon 880, §2). In either case, if the person survives and is no longer in danger of death, confirmation can be conferred at a later time, for example, on Pentecost Sunday, either by a bishop or by a presbyter who has the faculty (cf. RCIA, 24).

It must be stressed that it is *not* a sufficiently serious reason to delay confirmation merely to allow children to have more catechesis for confirmation or to enable them to be confirmed with older classmates. These pastoral considerations, while they appear to some ministers, parents and educators to have a certain merit, are not serious enough to overcome the important doctrinal, liturgical and canonical reasons for maintaining the integrity of the initiation rite and the proper sequence for reception of the sacraments. Moreover, if a child seven or older is judged to have adequate catechesis for baptism, *ipso facto* he or she has adequate catechesis for confirmation. Baptism is the more important of the two sacraments; it is necessary for salvation and makes one a member of the church (canon 849). Appropriately, the canonical requirements for preparation and catechesis for adult baptism are far more demanding than those for confirmation. For adult baptism, the law requires the lengthy period of the catechumenate and progression through its various stages (canon 851, 1°; RCIA, 253); for confirmation, the law merely requires that one be "suitably instructed, properly disposed and able to renew one's baptismal promises" (canon 889, §2). Thus, delaying confirmation in order to provide additional catechesis for confirmation not only is a violation of canon law and the liturgical books, it also may appear to diminish the primacy of baptism by implying that greater readiness and maturity is needed for confirmation than for baptism.

The NCCB Statutes state that when the diocesan bishop wants to reserve the celebration of confirmation to himself, he also should reserve adult baptisms and the rite of reception into full communion (NCCB Statutes, 13, 35). It is clear from this norm that the desire to preserve the bishop's role as ordinary minister of confirmation (canon 882) is of itself not a sufficient reason to delay confirmation after adult baptism or after the profession of faith of a baptized person seeking full communion.

6
MINISTERS

The liturgical law envisions a team approach in the formation of catechumens. Priests, deacons, catechists, sponsors, godparents and other members of the community are to be involved throughout the catechumenal process and in the celebration of the rites of initiation. Christian initiation is an *ecclesial* activity *par excellence*, involving various roles and ministries and at some points even the entire local community when possible. For example, RCIA, 121, §2, states:

> Before the rite of election the bishop, priests, deacons, catechists, godparents and the entire community, in accord with their respective responsibilities and in their own way, should, after considering the matter carefully, arrive at a judgment about the catechumens' state of formation and progress. After the election, they should surround the elect with prayer, so that the entire church will accompany and lead them to encounter Christ.

The catechumen is being welcomed into a community, the community of the parish, the diocese and the universal church; it is the community's leaders, teachers, and all its members, in varying degrees, who participate in the initiation process, assist the catechumens in their progress and judge their suitability for advancement (Cf. also *General Introduction to Christian Initiation*, 7; RCIA, 43).

MINISTERS of CHRISTIAN FORMATION

The team approach should characterize all aspects of the formation of catechumens: "The entire community should be involved in the formation of catechumens—priests, deacons, catechists, sponsors, godparents, friends and neighbors . . ." (RCIA, 80). Nevertheless, certain ministers have special roles in catechumenal formation.

BISHOPS

Diocesan bishops have the principal role of overseeing Christian formation and initiation in their dioceses. They are "the chief stewards of the mysteries of God and leaders of the entire liturgical life in the Church committed to them" (Cf. *General Introduction to Christian Initiation*, 12; *Christus Dominus*, 15; canons 756, §2; 835, §1).

PASTORS

It is at the level of the parish, not the diocese, that the Christian community typically gathers as community. Thus, parish ministers generally have a more immediate impact on the formation of Christians than the bishop does. The pastor oversees the pastoral care of a parish entrusted to him by authority of the bishop. He carries out the church's duties of teaching, sanctifying and governing in cooperation with other presbyters and with deacons and lay members of the faithful (cf. canons 519, 528, 529). The pastor is responsible for establishing a catechumenal program for adults seeking baptism and for overseeing the program in his parish (cf. canons 843, §2, and 851, 1°).

CATECHISTS

Although the pastor oversees the catechumenal program, he or the diocesan bishop usually appoints one or more catechists to instruct the catechumens and to assist in other ways in the formational process. A catechist in the law is a lay person. Priests and deacons, even those who are involved in catechetical ministry, are not called catechists.

In missionary territories, *catechist* has a specialized meaning. There it refers to an office held by a layperson who generally is a full-time minister of the church and who is often the leader of the local community in places where there are no resident clergy. These catechists receive a special formation for their apostolate, which they exercise under the supervision of missionaries (cf. canon 785).

MINISTERS of BLESSINGS, MINOR EXORCISMS and ANOINTINGS

Among the liturgical rites of the catechumenate are blessings, minor exorcisms and anointing with the oil of catechumens, all of which are sacramentals. The minister of sacramentals is a priest or deacon, and some sacramentals can be administered by authorized lay ministers (canon 1168). The anointing with the oil of catechumens can be done only by a priest or deacon. A priest, but not a deacon, may bless the oil when, for pastoral reasons, the oil blessed by the bishop is not used (RCIA, 101).

Presbyters can administer blessings, except for those reserved to the pope or to bishops (canon 1169, §2).[1] Deacons and lay persons can impart only those blessings permitted to them by law (cf. canon 1169, §3; *Book of Blessings, passim*).[2] The general rule is that if a minister may preside at a rite, he or she may give the blessing at that rite. For example, the presiding priest would give any blessings connected with Christian initiation that take place during the eucharist; a deacon who presides at a wedding would impart the nuptial blessing; a duly authorized catechist could give a blessing at the end of a celebration of the word at which he or she presides.

Priests and deacons may preside at the blessings and minor exorcisms of the catechumenate. However, only catechists who have been appointed by the bishop or his delegate may preside at these blessings and minor exorcisms (cf. RCIA, 12, 16, 96). Catechists appointed by the pastor may not give blessings unless the bishop has delegated to the pastor the competence to appoint them for this role.

MINISTERS OF THE SACRAMENTS OF INITIATION

The ordinary minister of baptism is a bishop, presbyter or deacon; a catechist or other person deputed for this function by the local ordinary may confer baptism lawfully, as can anyone in a case of necessity provided they have the proper intention, namely, to do what the church does when it baptizes (canon 861). However, because only a priest may preside at the latter rites of initiation, confirmation and eucharist, the minister for adult sacramental initiation must be a priest. Likewise, only a priest may preside at the rite of reception into full communion.

Adult sacramental initiation, including children of catechetical age, may be reserved to the diocesan bishop, if he wishes (canon 863; NCCB Statutes, 11). If the bishop is not the minister, the law expresses a preference for the pastor. Among the functions that are especially entrusted to the pastor is the administration of baptism (canon 530, 1°), which includes the sacramental initiation of adults.

In order to confirm validly, a presbyter must have the faculty by law or by special mandate of the bishop. Pastors and parochial vicars (assistant pastors), as well as other presbyters who have a pastoral office, such as chaplains, have the faculty to confirm by the law itself whenever they administer the sacraments of initiation to those who are seven or older, and have the use of reason, and whenever they receive a baptized person into full communion with the Catholic church. For persons in danger of death, any presbyter can confirm validly (canon 883).

Presbyters who have a pastoral office also have the faculty by law to confirm two categories of uncatechized adult Catholics: (a) baptized Catholics who had been apostate from the faith but are now returning to the Catholic faith; and (b) baptized Catholics who, through no fault of their own, were brought up in a non-Catholic religion (NCCB Statutes, 28). The law does not give the faculty for presbyters to confirm in the case of baptized Catholics who never practiced their faith. They never joined another church or apostasized; they simply never practiced their Catholic religion. For a presbyter validly to confirm uncatechized adults in this category, he must request the faculty from the diocesan bishop (NCCB Statutes, 29). It is also possible for the diocesan bishop to give general delegation to presbyters for cases of this kind.

A presbyter who does not have a pastoral office also may not validly confirm unless he has a mandate from the bishop. For example, a presbyter who teaches at a university wishes to preside at the rite of reception of a baptized non-Catholic into full communion with the Catholic church. To confirm validly at the rite, he must have a mandate from the bishop.[3]

A presbyter who does not have a pastoral office may not preside at the sacramental initiation of adults unless he has a mandate from the diocesan bishop. Without such a mandate, the confirmation would be invalid. The mandate to preside at adult initiation does not have to mention specifically any mandate to confirm; the mandate to baptize adults carries with it the mandate to confirm (NCCB Statutes, 12).

In the Eastern churches, confirmation always is conferred at baptism, even upon infants. If a Latin rite priest has the faculty to baptize members of an Eastern Catholic church, he also has the faculty to confirm them.[4] Unless he has bi-ritual faculties, the Latin priest must baptize and confirm the Eastern rite person, whether infant or adult, according to the liturgical books of the Latin church (canon 846, §2).

Whenever a priest has the faculty to confirm, whether by law or by special mandate, he *must* use it (canon 885, §2; NCCB Statutes, 13). The administration of confirmation is not optional at the initiation of those who are seven or older, and have the use of reason. Likewise, confirmation is not optional at the baptism of Eastern rite persons, even infants.

ENDNOTES

1. A presbyter in canon law is a priest who is not a bishop. A bishop is a priest who is not a presbyter. "Priest" is a generic term which applies to both presbyters and bishops.

2. Lists of blessings that can be given by deacons and lay persons is found in John Huels, *The Pastoral Companion: A Canon Law Handbook for Catholic Ministry* (Chicago: Franciscan Herald Press, 1986), pp. 265–67.

3. In such a case, the church would not supply the faculty due to common error. However, if the priest were resident in the rectory of the parish where the confirmation took place, the church would supply the faculty in virtue of common error. For further discussion of the supplied faculty, see The Pastoral Companion, pp.64–65.

4. See *Code of Canons of the Eastern Churches: Latin-English Edition* (Washington: Canon Law Society of America, 1990), canon 696, §2.

7
SPONSORS AND GODPARENTS

The ministries of sponsor and godparent are distinct for adult initiation, although they may be done by the same person. The English vernacular translation in the official liturgical book renders the Latin *sponsor* as "sponsor" and *patrinus* as "godparent." Sometimes the Latin word *patrinus* is also rendered "sponsor" in English, as it is in the version of the Code of Canon Law published by the Canon Law Society of America. The official translation in the approved liturgical books, however, is "godparent"; this term is preferable because it clearly distinguishes between the two different roles. The ministry of the sponsor need not be fulfilled by the same person as the canonical *patrinus*.

SPONSOR

The presence of a sponsor for each candidate is required at the rite of acceptance into the order of catechumens. Often this sponsor is later chosen by the catechumen to be his or her godparent for the rite of election and for sacramental initiation. But it sometimes happens that the two persons are different, as, for example, when the one who is going to be the official godparent is unable to attend the rite of acceptance into the order of catechumens or is unable to participate in the early stages of the catechumenate.

The qualifications of the sponsor for the rite of acceptance into the order of catechumens are not demanding. The sponsor must know the candidate, help him or her, and witness to the candidate's morals, faith and intention (RCIA, 10). The sponsor need not fulfill the other qualifications of the canonical godparent. It is desirable, if possible, that the canonical godparents also be the sponsors during the rite of admission to the catechumenate. In this rite the sponsors acknowledge their readiness to help the catechumens come to know and follow Christ, and they testify that the catechumens have chosen Christ as Lord and wish to serve him.

GODPARENTS

The godparent plays a major role in adult initiation, beginning in the catechumenate. He or she is to be close to the catechumen, a friend, one whose example and character is a model of Christian life for the catechumen (RCIA, 11). The duties of godparents for adult initiation can be considered in three phases: the period of the catechumenate, the celebration of the sacraments of initiation and the postbaptismal relationship.

The public office of godparent begins at the rite of election, when the church hears the godparents' testimony concerning the suitability of the catechumens. They testify to the Christian community that the catechumens have faithfully listened to the word of God, have been true to that word, have begun to walk in God's presence, have sought the fellowship of their brothers and sisters, have joined them in prayer and are worthy of admission to the sacraments of initiation. The godparents are exhorted by the presider to continue helping the catechumens by their loving care and example. Throughout the catechumenate the godparents are to "show the candidates how to practice the gospel in personal and social life and to sustain them in moments of hesitancy and anxiety" (RCIA, 11).

During the celebration of the sacraments of initiation, the godparents take an active role comparable to that of the parents at infant baptism. The godparent informs the presider of the name of the candidate, touches the candidate during or immediately after the immersion or infusion of water and presents the newly baptized person with a candle lighted from the Easter candle.

In the period of mystagogia, the godparents continue to play an important role by helping the neophytes become included into the life of the community and by accompanying them to Sunday Mass. There also is an ongoing responsibility the godparents have of assisting the neophytes to remain faithful to their baptismal promises. Ideally the special spiritual relationship between godparent and neophyte will last throughout their lives. The lifelong role of godparents is specified more by family or local custom than it is by canon law. The code states only that the godparent "will help the baptized to lead a Christian life in harmony with baptism and to fulfill faithfully the obligations connected with it" (canon 872).

QUALIFICATIONS of GODPARENTS

NUMBER and SEX

Ordinarily there should be one godparent for each catechumen, male or female; or there can be two godparents, one godmother and one godfather (canon 873). This excludes two godparents of the same sex or more than two godparents. In a case of necessity when no one is available to assume the role of godparent, anyone with the proper intention can baptize, but he or she should try to have at least one witness present who could testify to the fact that the baptism was validly conferred (canon 875). The proper intention is simply to do what the church does when it baptizes. Anyone with the use of reason can function as a witness.

In some places it is customary to have two godparents at infant baptism and only one godparent for adult initiation, but there is nothing to prevent having two godparents for an adult or only one for an infant. The catechumens themselves should be free to determine whether they want one godparent or two.

DESIGNATION and APPROVAL

Godparents must have the intention of performing their role; that is, they must intend to assume an ongoing spiritual relationship with the baptized person and not merely function as a passive witness to the sacrament. In adult initiation the godparents are chosen by the person to be baptized, and they must be approved by the local priest with, insofar as possible, the acceptance of the Christian community (canon 874, §1, 1°; RCIA, 11, 123). Given the importance of the godparents in the process of adult initiation, only faithful Catholics who are fitting models of the Christian life should be approved for this role.

AGE

Godparents must be *at least sixteen*, unless the diocesan bishop has established another age or unless in an exceptional case it seems to the pastor or minister that there is just cause to admit a younger person (canon 874, §1, 2°). An example of a just cause for admitting a younger person would be a close personal or familial relationship. In such cases, those who are fourteen or fifteen could be godparents provided they meet all the other legal qualifications.

In reference to baptism, those fourteen and older have a special place in canon law. The rites for "Christian Initiation of Children Who Have Reached Catechetical Age" (RCIA, 252–330) are to be followed for all who have the use of reason, which legally is presumed to be attained around the age of seven. However, those who are fourteen and older can choose their own rite of baptism, either the Latin rite or an Eastern rite Catholic church (canon 111, §2), and they are to be referred to the bishop so that he may celebrate their sacramental initiation if he judges it expedient (canon 863). Fourteen was the standard minimal age to be a godparent in the law of the 1917 code. It also is the age at which a woman can marry validly in the church (men must be sixteen; cf. canon 1083). Because the age of fourteen indicates in the law the attainment of a certain degree of maturity, and because the role of godparent is that of a mature Christian, it does not seem advisable, even with good reason, to approve a godparent who is younger than fourteen.

FULLY INITIATED CATHOLICS

Godparents must be Catholic, whether of the Latin rite or an Eastern rite, and they must have received the sacraments of confirmation and eucharist (canon 874, §1, 3°). A Catholic is anyone who has been baptized into the Catholic church or who has been received into full communion with it.

The *Directory for Ecumenism*, 98b, provides one exception to this rule, namely, for separated Eastern Christians. A suitable Eastern non-Catholic can be a godparent at the baptism of a Catholic, provided there is also a Catholic godparent designated and as long as the Catholic upbringing of the one to be baptized is assured. Reciprocally, a Catholic can be a godparent at a baptism in a separated Eastern church along with an Eastern non-Catholic godparent. In either case, the responsibility for seeing to the Christian upbringing of the baptized person belongs primarily to the godparent who belongs to the church in which the person was baptized.

Protestants may not be godparents at the baptism of a Catholic, but a validly baptized Protestant can be admitted and recorded as a *witness* together with the Catholic godparent (canon 874, §2). Protestants are treated differently in canon law than Eastern non-Catholics because the latter are considered to be more closely in communion with the Catholic church than Protestants are.

IN GOOD STANDING

Godparents must lead a life of faith in harmony with the undertaking of their role (canon 874, §1, 3°). Explicitly excluded from being a godparent is anyone who has incurred a canonical penalty that has been lawfully imposed or declared by competent ecclesiastical authority (canon 874, §1, 4°).

Often it is difficult in large parishes for the priest or other minister who is asked to certify the good standing of godparents to know who truly is living a life of faith in harmony with this role. Often the best way to assure that this requirement is met is to impress upon the catechumens the necessity of choosing a proper model as godparent; then the parish priest will be in a better position to trust their judgment and not doubt the suitability of the person chosen.

NOT A PARENT

A godparent may not be the father or mother of the person being baptized. This requirement applies more to infant baptism than adult initiation, but it is also applicable in the case of the initiation of a child of catechetical age. The roles of the parents and godparents are distinct. Christian parents have the primary responsibility for the Christian upbringing of their children; the godparents serve in an auxiliary role except when neither parent is Catholic.

There is nothing in the Latin rite canon law to prevent spouses, clergy or religious from being godparents, as there was in the law previous to the 1983 code. The Eastern Catholic churches, however, prohibit a spouse as well as parents from being godparents.[1]

CONFIRMATION

Candidates for reception into full communion with the Catholic church are to be accompanied by a sponsor and may even have two sponsors. The Latin original uses the word *sponsor* here, not *patrinus*, and the English translation is rendered "sponsor" (RCIA, 483). Because this does not refer to the godparent (*patrinus*), it is unnecessary that all the qualifications for a godparent be met by the sponsor at the rite of reception. It would be sufficient to have a suitable Catholic who is fully initiated and willing to undertake this role. If anyone has had a principal part in guiding or preparing the candidate, he or she should be designated as the sponsor (RCIA, 483).

ENDNOTES

1. Code of Canons of the Eastern Churches, canon 685, §1, 5°.

8
RECORD KEEPING

The church has long been concerned with maintaining accurate records of important facts about its members. Comprehensive and up-to-date record books are necessary to provide information about and authentication of ecclesial statuses and events. For example, proof of baptism and confirmation is necessary in order to be a godparent (canons 874, §1, 3°; 893, §1), to enter the novitiate (canon 645, §1) or the seminary (canon 241, §2), to be ordained (canon 1050, 3°) and to be married (canons 1065, 1068, 1086). The parish record books in churches around the world are also an extremely valuable and frequently unique source of personal and social data for historians and archivists. With such values in mind, the legislator imposes on the pastor the principal obligation of overseeing the maintenance of the parish registers.

> Each parish is to possess a set of parish books including baptismal, marriage and death registers as well as other registers prescribed by the conference of bishops or the diocesan bishop; the pastor is to see to it that these registers are accurately inscribed and carefully preserved. (canon 535, §1)

When the pastor is sick or dying, the law obliges the vicar forane, or dean, to see that the parish books are not lost or taken elsewhere (canon 555, §3).

BAPTISMAL REGISTER

The most important parish book is the baptismal register. It is the permanent record of each Catholic; it includes information about the reception of certain other sacraments and changes of ecclesial status throughout the course of a person's life. Besides information pertinent to one's baptism, the baptismal register also contains a notation of the person's confirmation and whatever affects his or her canonical status by way of marriage, adoption, reception of holy orders, perpetual profession in a religious institute and change of rite. These notations should always be included on a baptismal certificate whenever one is issued (canon 535, §2). Each parish is required to have a registry or archive where the parish books are kept along with episcopal letters and other documents. The pastor is bound to take care of them and to see that outsiders do not get hold of them; he is to be especially careful with the older parish books, which are more valuable for historical purposes. The bishop or his delegate is obliged to inspect the parish books during his canonical visitation or at some other time (cf. canon 535, §§4 and 5).

The pastor of the place where the baptism is celebrated has the duty of seeing that the pertinent data are recorded carefully and without delay. If the baptism was administered neither by the pastor nor in his presence, the minister of baptism must inform the pastor of the parish where baptism was administered so that he may record it (canon 878).

The law requires the following to be noted in the baptismal register: the names of those baptized, the minister, parents, godparents, witnesses (if there were any), the place and date of celebration, and the date and place of birth (canon 877, §1). In the case of a child born of an unwed mother, the name of the mother is inserted if there is public proof of her maternity or if she requests this either in writing or orally before two witnesses. The name of the father of a child born out of wedlock is recorded if his paternity has been proven either by some public document or by his own declaration before the pastor and two witnesses. In other such cases, no mention is made of the parents' names (cf. canon 877, §2). When an adopted child is baptized, the names of the adopting parents are recorded. The names of the natural parents are to be recorded at least when this must be done in the civil records of the region, in keeping with canon 877, §§1 and 2, and with due regard for any norms that the episcopal conference of a region might have issued (cf. canon 877, §3). These provisions of the law are applicable to both adult and infant baptism (cf. *General Introduction to Christian Initiation*, 29).

CONFIRMATION RECORD

The pastor of the place where confirmation is celebrated is obliged to notify the pastor of the place of baptism about the conferral of confirmation so that it can be noted in the baptismal register. If the pastor was not present for the confirmation, the minister either personally or through another is to inform the pastor of the confirmation as soon as possible (cf. canons 895 and 896; *Rite of Confirmation*, 14–15). A confirmation register also is kept in the diocesan curia (canon 895); the appropriate diocesan official should be informed by the pastor or other minister whenever confirmation is celebrated. This duty should be especially heeded when confirmation is conferred by a presbyter in the case of adult initiation, reception into full communion or danger of death. In keeping with local custom, the requirements of the episcopal conference of a region or the requirements of the diocesan bishop, there might also be a confirmation register kept in the parish archives. In this book are recorded the names of those confirmed in the parish, the minister, the parents and the sponsors, and the date and place of conferral (cf. canon 895; *Rite of Confirmation*, 14).

OTHER REGISTERS

Besides the registers of baptism and confirmation, the RCIA calls for three additional record books: the register of catechumens, the book of the elect and a book for recording the names of baptized Christians who have been received into the full communion of the Catholic church.

REGISTER OF CATECHUMENS

The register of catechumens is simply a book that principally records the names of catechumens who have been formally accepted into the catechumenate in accord with the rite of acceptance into the order of catechumens of the RCIA. Upon acceptance into the catechumenate by means of this rite, a person takes on the recognized status of a catechumen in the church, is entitled to the rights and is bound by the obligations of a catechumen as discussed earlier. It is important to keep an up-to-date record of the names of all catechumens because they have a public status in the church, even though they are not yet members of the faithful. In addition to the names of the catechumens, the register should contain the names of the sponsors, the minister of the rite of acceptance, and the date and place of the celebration of the rite (RCIA, 46).

BOOK OF THE ELECT

The book of the elect records the names of catechumens who are entering the final step before sacramental initiation, the period of purification and enlightenment, which is begun by the rite of election. This step of the catechumenate is sometimes called "the enrollment of names" because "as a pledge of fidelity the candidates inscribe their names in the book that lists those who have been chosen for initiation" (RCIA, 119). The names are entered in the book during the rite itself, and it can be done in various ways. The candidates may inscribe their names themselves, or they may call out their names, to be inscribed by the godparents or by the priest in charge of the catechumens' initiation, or by a deacon, a catechist, or a representative of the community who presented the candidates earlier in the rite. If there are a great many candidates, the enrollment may simply consist in the presentation of a list of names to the celebrant. As an alternative, the names may be inscribed in the book before the celebration of the rite of election when the optional rite of the sending of the catechumens for election is chosen (cf. RCIA, 113, 130, 132, 553). The godparents also may write their names along with the catechumens in the book of the elect (RCIA, 123). When children of catechetical age are being initiated, the rite of election is optional. If this option is chosen, the names are inscribed in one of the same ways as in the case of adults (cf. RCIA, 284).

REGISTER OF THOSE RECEIVED INTO FULL COMMUNION

The law states that the book for recording the names of baptized Christians who have been received into the full communion of the Catholic church is to be a special book, that is, one different from other registers. When such a book is lacking, however, the intent of the law would be satisfied if the specified information were to be recorded in a designated part of the baptismal register.

Because those received into full communion were not baptized in the Catholic church, this register is their book of permanent record in the church, equivalent to the baptismal register for those baptized Catholic. In addition to the names of those received into full communion, the date and place of their baptism also are to be noted in it (RCIA, 486). It would also be desirable to record the names of the minister of baptism, the parents and the godparents, and the date and place of birth in order to have more complete information readily available if it should be needed later. Those who were not validly confirmed in their previous ecclesial community are confirmed during this rite, and their confirmation should be duly recorded in the proper books.

When parents of baptized children below the age of discretion are received into full communion, they usually wish to have the children become Catholic also. In that case, the names of the children and all other information already noted should be recorded in the register. Although these children are not capable of making the profession of faith in accord with the rite, the faith of the parents suffices, as it does at infant baptism. By recording this information, these children will have a permanent record and proof of their membership in the Catholic church. Children who have the use of reason can be treated as adults when being received into full communion, as they are at baptism. They are capable of making the profession of faith and can freely decide for themselves whether they wish to become a Catholic.

9
MARRIAGE CASES

Ordinarily, a wedding in the Catholic church can be celebrated only when one or both parties is Catholic (cf. canons 1109–1110). Among the privileges of being a catechumen is the right to celebrate one's marriage in the church. This right extends to two catechumens who wish to marry and to a catechumen who wishes to marry an unbaptized person (RCIA, 47). No dispensation from the impediment of disparity of cult (canon 1086, §2) is necessary in these cases because neither party is Catholic. Likewise, in such a case the catechumen is not required to make the declaration to remove dangers of falling away from the faith and the promise to do all in his or her power to have the children baptized and brought up in the Catholic church, which are requirements for mixed marriages (canon 1125, 1°).

When a catechumen marries a Catholic it is treated as a disparity of cult marriage, and the dispensation from that impediment is required. In such a marriage the declaration and promise to be made by the Catholic party in a mixed marriage is technically required, although not for the validity of the dispensation (canon 1086, §2). It would be desirable, however, to omit this usual promise and declaration whenever a Catholic marries a catechumen. The reason is that the law was not intended for this case. The catechumen already is a member of Christ's household, one who desires to become a Christian, and therefore it should be presumed that the catechumen would neither pose a danger to the faith of the Catholic party nor prevent the children from being baptized and raised Catholic. To require the usual precautions for a mixed marriage in the case of a catechumen and a Catholic would likely be insulting to both parties.

Although the universal law does not mention the case of a catechumen marrying a baptized non-Catholic in the Catholic church, this is permitted by the NCCB Statutes, 10. Because neither party is Catholic, neither the dispensation from disparity of cult nor the formalities for mixed marriage (canons 1124–1125) are required.

Whenever a catechumen is married in the Catholic church, chapter III of the *Rite of Marriage*, "Rite for Celebrating Marriage between a Catholic and an Unbaptized Person," is to be used. In the 1991 *editio typica altera* of the *Ordo Celebrandi Matrimonium*, which at this time is not yet available in English, it is the fourth rite, the "Rite for Celebrating Marriage between a Catholic Party and a Catechumen or a Non-Christian Party." It is forbidden to celebrate such marriages at the eucharistic liturgy. The nuptial blessing in chapter I, n. 33, of the ritual may be used, but all references to eucharistic sharing are to be omitted (NCCB Statutes, 10). Communion should not be given even to the Catholic participants at a wedding without Mass, not only because communion ordinarily should be distributed only during Mass (canon 918) but also because the eucharist is preeminently a sign of unity; when only one spouse or one part of the assembly can receive, the sign conveyed is one of disunity and separation.

The marriage between a catechumen and a baptized person is not a sacrament. Only baptized persons can validly receive any sacrament (canon 842, §1), and both parties to a marriage must be baptized for it to be a sacramental marriage. When the catechumen already married to a baptized person is him- or herself baptized, that marriage becomes a sacrament at the moment of baptism. By definition, any valid marriage between two baptized persons is a sacrament (canon 1055, §2). It is neither necessary nor desirable to renew consent or in some other way celebrate this marriage again after the baptism, because it was presumably a valid marriage from the beginning and consent is presumed to continue (canons 1060 and 1107). Thus, a new wedding ceremony might be confusing to some and might suggest that the couple had not been validly married.

While catechumens have a right to marry in a Catholic church ceremony, they are not obliged to do so. The marriages of two catechumens and those of a catechumen with a non-Catholic are canonically valid no matter where or how they take place, provided the marriages are valid according to the civil law that is in effect where the marriage takes place (canon 22), and provided that the parties validly consent and are not bound by an impediment of the divine law.

The marriage of a catechumen and a Catholic must be celebrated according to the canonical form for the validity of the marriage, that is, before a Catholic priest or deacon who has the faculty to assist at marriages and before two other witnesses (canon 1108). Those bound to the canonical form are all Catholics who were baptized in the Catholic church or who were received into it and have not left it by a formal act (canon 1117).

Examples of a formal act of leaving the church are: a Catholic who registers in a non-Catholic church with the intention of abandoning the Catholic faith and becoming a member of the non-Catholic church; or a Catholic who states in writing or before witnesses that he or she has left the Catholic church. Mere non-practice of the Catholic religion, no matter for how long a duration, does not excuse from the observance of the canonical form. A Catholic who has formally left the church, although technically still a Catholic (canon 11), is not bound by the canonical form, and thus the marriage of a catechumen to such an ex-Catholic would be valid under the same conditions as for a marriage between any two non-Catholics as given in the preceding paragraph.

IRREGULAR MARRIAGES

A frequently occurring pastoral problem in the experience of those who direct the initiation process on the local level is the presence of persons who are desirous of becoming Christians but who are in an irregular marriage. Because they, or their present spouse, or perhaps both of them were previously married, and the previous spouse is still living, they are bound by the divine-law impediment of prior bond (canon 1085), and consequently their present marriage is canonically invalid. This often poses a dilemma because, while persons in invalid marriages may become catechumens, they are unable to complete the process by receiving the sacraments of initiation.[1] They may, however, receive all three sacraments of initiation when in danger of death, making the profession of faith and the promises contained in *Pastoral Care of the Sick: Rite of Anointing and Viaticum*, "Christian Initiation for the Dying" (cf. n. 282).

To deal adequately with the problem of inquirers or catechumens who are in irregular second marriages, it is important for those in charge of Christian initiation on the local level to avoid a "programmatic" attitude toward the catechumenate. Such a view considers Christian initiation as a parish program or course, with regular sessions lasting several months or a year, after which all participants are expected to have uniformly appropriated their formation in order to be ready to receive the sacraments of initiation together at the Easter Vigil. Instead, it is better to describe Christian initiation as a process that is geared to the living realities of individuals whose status, circumstances and needs are various and whose growth in faith and response to the gospel proceed at different paces. The *praenotanda* to the RCIA envision a catechumenate process that may take several years and that does not inevitably lead to sacramental initiation.

> The duration of the catechumenate will depend on the grace of God and on various circumstances. . . . Nothing can be determined a priori. The time spent in the catechumenate should be long enough—several years if necessary—for conversion and faith of the catechumens to become strong. (RCIA, 76)

No one can be forced to accept the faith against his or her will (canon 748, §2), but neither can anyone claim a right to sacramental initiation when the church determines that he or she is not ready (cf. canon 843, §2). In reference to adult initiation, readiness is determined by the local community and its leaders (RCIA, 118–125), and this judgment is based on the circumstances of each individual, including the canonical status of his or her marriage.

When ministers, catechists and catechumens accept from the beginning that the catechumenate is a process that does not automatically result in initiation at the next Easter Vigil but may take as long as needed for the individuals in it, then the problem of catechumens who are in irregular marriages will not seem so pressing. There will be ample time to prepare and await the results of an annulment or dissolution procedure, provided that this procedure is begun as soon as possible.

Pastoral ministers and catechists must be prepared to deal in general fashion with questions relative to the church's doctrine and canon law on marriage from the outset of the catechumenal process. Already in the precatechumenate, or period of inquiry, the responsible persons for directing the Christian initiation on the local level should ascertain the marital status of all adult candidates to determine whether there were any previous marriages among the inquirers or their spouses. If so, the persons in question should be made aware as early as possible of the church's teaching on marriage. It should be made clear to them that the church does not accept civil divorce because of Christ's command in the gospel that what God has joined together in marriage cannot be broken by anyone (cf. Matthew 19:6; Mark 10:9). They should be taught that only by means of an ecclesiastical annulment or dissolution of the previous marriage is it possible for a subsequent marriage to be recognized by the church as valid. Such instruction should be given sensitively and nonjudgmentally, adapted to the capacities of the inquirers to understand and taking care that they not be alienated from their intention to pursue the path of Christian initiation.

In order to give proper instruction to such persons, catechists and ministers need to be familiar with the church's teaching on marriage, have some knowledge of the general method for proceeding toward marital annulment and dissolution, and also be aware of the way that such specific cases are handled in their own dioceses. Various procedures exist for regularizing marriages according to the circumstances. When the catechumen's previous spouse is unbaptized, dissolution by means of the Pauline privilege is the likely solution, a procedure that is completed on the diocesan level without the need to petition the Apostolic See (cf. canons 1143–1147). If the previous spouse is baptized, the so-called Petrine privilege might be applicable whereby the pope dissolves the bond of the previous marriage in favor of the faith of the party who wishes to be baptized. Although rare, there also are cases in which a dissolution is granted by the pope due to the lack of consummation of the previous marriage (canon 1142). Unlike the Pauline privilege and annulments, the Petrine privilege and nonconsummation cases require adjudication by the Holy See and therefore often take longer before a decision is obtained.

Any person, baptized or unbaptized, may petition the proper diocesan tribunal for a declaration of nullity of his or her marriage (cf. canons 1476 and 1674, 1°). Although non-Catholics are not bound by ecclesiastical law (and thus are not bound to the canonical form or to the impediments of ecclesiastical law), the church has the power to annul their marriages because all people are subject to the divine law. Thus they are bound to give valid consent to their marriage, since consent is of the essence of marriage (canon 1057), whether this be Christian or natural marriage; and they are bound by impediments of the divine law, among which is the impediment of prior bond. Indeed, the most frequent basis on which church tribunals judge that a previous marriage of an unbaptized person was juridically null and void is some kind of defective consent, the same ground for nullity that is most frequent for marriages of Catholics and baptized non-Catholics.

In explaining the annulment or dissolution process to inquirers or catechumens, pastoral ministers and catechists should strive to eliminate fears and misconceptions about these procedures from the very beginning. It is helpful to explain that a declaration of nullity does not mean that the person's previous marriage never existed on the existential level. Rather, the annulment proceeding looks to the circumstances and condition of the parties and their marriage to determine if the marriage was juridically defective from the beginning on the basis of what the church teaches marriage should be. Many people also fear that an annulment implies that their children will be considered illegitimate. To counter this misconception it should be a regular part of the catechesis on the church's doctrine of marriage to tell the catechumens in question that an annulment has no effect on the legitimacy of their children (cf. canons 1137 and 1061, §3).

CONVALIDATION

Once a dissolution or annulment of the previous marriage or marriages has been obtained, the catechumen who had been in an irregular union is now canonically free to be elected in the rite of enrollment of names and to proceed toward sacramental initiation. If the catechumen's present spouse is non-Catholic, it is unnecessary to convalidate the marriage because renewal of consent is a requirement of the ecclesiastical law only (canon 1156, §2). It is not required by the natural law because the consent given in the beginning of marriage and not later revoked is still effective (canon 1107).

When the catechumen's present spouse is Catholic, however, it is necessary to have the marriage convalidated by means of a public renewal of consent according to the canonical form (canon 1158, §1). This should be done as soon as possible after notification of the annulment or dissolution, and before the Christian initiation of the catechumen. It is preferable that the convalidation take place without solemnity before the local ordinary or pastor, or properly delegated priest or deacon, and before two witnesses. Only that part of the marriage ritual need be observed which pertains to the essence of marriage, namely, the consent of the parties and the asking for the consent and receiving it in the name of the church by the presiding priest or deacon (cf. *Rite of Marriage*, 60–61; nn. 161–163 in the 1991 *Ordo Celebrandi Matrimonium*).

ENDNOTES

1. Cf. Congregation for the Doctrine of the Faith, reply, July 11, 1983, *Canon Law Digest*, vol. 10, ed. James I. O'Connor (Mundelein, Ill.: 1986), pages 139–140. The document also appears in *Roman Replies 1983*, ed. William Schumacher (Washington, D.C.: Canon Law Society of America, 1983), pages 2–3.

APPENDIX A

RECOMMENDED READING

The Code of Canon Law: A Text and Commentary Commissioned by the Canon Law Society of America. Edited by James Coriden, Thomas Green and Donald Heintschel. New York/Mahwah: Paulist Press, 1985.

Gaupin, Linda. "RCIA: Canonical Issues, A Liturgical Response." In *Canon Law Society of America Proceedings of the Forty-sixth Annual Convention,* 130–40. Washington, DC: Canon Law Society of America, 1985.

Huels, John. *Liturgical Law: An Introduction.* Washington, DC: The Pastoral Press, 1987.

Huels, John. *The Pastoral Companion: A Canon Law Handbook for Catholic Ministry.* Chicago: Franciscan Herald Press, 1986.

Jarrell, Lynn. "Canonical Issues Surrounding the Sacraments of Initiation." In *Canon Law Society of America Proceedings of the Fifty-Fifth Annual Convention,* 167–83. Washington, DC: Canon Law Society of America, 1993.

APPENDIX B

TEXTS of CANONS CITED

Canon 7—A law comes into existence when it is promulgated.

Canon 8—§1. Universal ecclesiastical laws are promulgated by being published in the official commentary *Acta Apostolicae Sedis* unless another form of promulgation is prescribed for individual cases. These laws become effective only after three months have elapsed from the date of that issue of the *Acta,* unless they have binding force immediately from the very nature of the matter they treat or unless the law itself specifically and expressly suspends its force for a shorter or longer period.

§2. Particular laws are promulgated in a manner determined by the legislator, and they begin to bind one month from the date of promulgation, unless another time period is determined in the law itself.

Canon 9—Laws deal with the future and not the past, unless specific provision be made in the laws concerning the past.

Canon 10—Only those laws which expressly state that an act is null or that a person is incapable of acting are to be considered to be invalidating or incapacitating.

Canon 11—Merely ecclesiastical laws bind those baptized in the Catholic Church or received into it and who enjoy the sufficient use of reason and, unless the law expressly provides otherwise, have completed seven years of age.

Canon 12—§1. All persons for whom universal laws were passed are bound by them everywhere.

§2. However, all persons who are actually present in a certain territory are exempted from the universal laws which do not have force in that territory.

§3. With due regard for the prescription of can. 13, laws established for a particular territory bind those for whom they were passed when these persons have a domicile or a quasi-domicile there and are likewise actually present in the territory.

Canon 13—§1. Particular laws are not presumed to be personal but territorial, unless it is otherwise evident.

§2. Travelers:
>1° are not bound by the particular laws of their own territory as long as they are absent from it unless their violation would cause harm in their own territory or unless the laws are personal ones;
>2° are not bound by the laws of the territory in which they are present with the exception of those laws which provide for public order, which determine the formalities of legal actions, or which deal with immovable goods situated in that territory.

§3. Transients (*vagi*) are bound by both universal laws and the particular laws which are in force in the place where they are present.

Canon 14—When there is a doubt of law, laws do not bind even if they be nullifying and disqualifying ones. When there is doubt in fact, however, ordinaries can dispense from them. In the latter case, if it is a question of a reserved dispensation, the ordinaries can dispense so long as the dispensation is usually granted by the authority to whom it is reserved.

Canon 15—§1. Ignorance or error concerning invalidating or incapacitating laws does not hinder their effectiveness unless it is expressly determined otherwise.

§2. Ignorance or error about a law, a penalty, a fact concerning oneself, or a notorious fact concerning another is not presumed; it is presumed about a fact concerning another which is not notorious until the contrary is proven.

Canon 16—§1. Laws are authentically interpreted by the legislator and by the one to whom the legislator has granted the power to interpret them authentically.

§2. An authentic interpretation communicated in the form of a law has the same force as the law itself and must be promulgated. Furthermore, if such an interpretation merely declares what was certain in the words of the law in themselves, it has retroactive force; if it restricts or extends the law or if it explains a doubtful law, it is not retroactive.

§3. However, an interpretation contained in a judicial decision or an administrative act in a particular matter does not have the force of law and binds only the persons and affects only those matters for which it was given.

Canon 17—Ecclesiastical laws are to be understood in accord with the proper meaning of the words considered in their text and context. If the meaning remains doubtful and obscure, recourse is to be taken to parallel passages, if such exist, to the purpose and the circumstances of the law, and to the mind of the legislator.

Canon 18—Laws which establish a penalty or restrict the free exercise of rights or which contain an exception to the law are subject to a strict interpretation.

Canon 19—Unless it is a penal matter, if an express prescription of universal or particular law or a custom is lacking in some particular matter, the case is to be decided in light of laws passed in similar circumstances, the general principles of law observed with canonical equity, the jurisprudence and praxis of the Roman Curia, and the common and constant opinion of learned persons.

Canon 20—A later law abrogates a former law or derogates from it if it expressly states so, if it is directly contrary to it, or if it entirely re-orders the subject matter of the former law; but a universal law in no way derogates from a particular or special law unless the law itself expressly provides otherwise.

Canon 21—In a case of doubt the revocation of a pre-existent law is not presumed, but later laws are to be related to earlier ones and, insofar as it is possible, harmonized with them.

Canon 22—Civil laws to which the law of the Church defers should be observed in canon law with the same effects, insofar as they are not contrary to divine law and unless it is provided otherwise in canon law.

Canon 96—By baptism one is incorporated into the Church of Christ and is constituted a person in it with duties and rights which are proper to Christians, in keeping with their condition, to the extent that they are in ecclesiastical communion and unless a legitimately issued sanction stands in the way.

Canon 97—§1. A person who has completed the eighteenth year of age is an adult; below this age, a person is a minor.

§2. Before the completion of the seventh year a minor is called to be an infant and is held to be incompetent (*non sui compos*); with the completion of the seventh year one is presumed to have the use of reason.

Canon 102—§1. Domicile is acquired by residence within the territory of a certain parish or at least of a diocese, which either is joined with the intention of remaining there permanently unless called away, or has been protracted for five complete years.

§2. Quasi-domicile is acquired by residence within the territory of a certain parish or at least of a diocese which either is joined with the intention of remaining there at least three months, unless called away, or has in fact been protracted for three months.

§3. A domicile or quasi-domicile within the territory of a parish is called parochial; in the territory of a diocese, even though not in a particular parish, it is called diocesan.

Canon 111—§1. A child of parents who belong to the Latin Church is ascribed to it by reception of baptism, or, if one or the other parent does not belong to the Latin Church and both parents agree in choosing that the child be baptized in the Latin Church, the child is ascribed to it by reception of baptism; but, if the agreement is lacking, the child is ascribed to the Ritual Church to which the father belongs.

§2. Anyone to be baptized who has completed the fourteenth year of age can freely choose to be baptized in the Latin Church or in another Ritual Church *sui iuris*, and in this case the person belongs to that Church which is chosen.

Canon 112—1. After the reception of baptism, the following are enrolled in another Ritual Church *sui iuris*:
  1° one who has obtained permission from the Apostolic See;
  2° a spouse who declares at the time of marriage or during marriage that he or she is transferring to the Ritual Church *sui iuris* of the other spouse; but when the marriage has ended, that person can freely return to the Latin Church;
  3° children of those in nn. 1 and 2 under fourteen complete years of age; and similarly children of a Catholic party in a mixed marriage who legitimately transferred to another Ritual Church. But, when such persons reach fourteen complete years of age, they may return to the Latin Church.

§2. The custom, however prolonged, of receiving the sacraments according to the rite of another Ritual Church *sui iuris*, does not carry with it enrollment in that Church.

Canon 135—§1. The power of governance is distinguished as legislative, executive and judicial.

§2. Legislative power is to be exercised in the manner prescribed by law, and that legislative power in the Church possessed by a legislator below the highest authority cannot be validly delegated, unless otherwise explicitly provided for in the law; a law which is contrary to a higher law cannot be validly enacted by a lower level legislator.

§3. Judicial power, which is possessed by judges or judicial colleges, is to be exercised in the manner prescribed by law and cannot be delegated, except to carry out acts which are preparatory to a decree or a decision.

§4. In regard to the exercise of executive power, the prescriptions of the following canons [as given in the complete text of the Code of Canon Law] are to be observed.

Canon 204—§1. The Christian faithful are those who, inasmuch as they have been incorporated in Christ through baptism, have been constituted as the people of God; for this reason, since they have become sharers in Christ's priestly, prophetic and royal office in their own manner, they are called to exercise the mission which God has entrusted to the Church to fulfill in the world, in accord with the condition proper to each one.

§2. This Church, constituted and organized as a society in this world, subsists in the Catholic Church, governed by the successor of Peter and the bishops in communion with him.

Canon 205—Those baptized are fully in communion with the Catholic Church on this earth who are joined with Christ in its visible structure by the bonds of profession of faith, of the sacraments and of ecclesiastical governance.

Canon 206—§1. Catechumens are in union with the Church in a special manner, that is, under the influence of the Holy Spirit, they ask to be incorporated into the Church by explicit choice and are therefore united with the Church by that choice just as by a life of faith, hope and charity which they lead; the Church already cherishes them as its own.

§2. The Church has special care for catechumens; the Church invites them to lead the evangelical life and introduces them to the celebration of sacred rites, and grants them various prerogatives which are proper to Christians.

Canon 213—The Christian faithful have the right to receive assistance from the sacred pastors out of the spiritual goods of the Church, especially the word of God and the sacraments.

Canon 225—§1. Since the laity like all the Christian faithful, are deputed by God to the apostolate through their baptism and confirmation, they are therefore bound by the general obligations and enjoy the general right to work as individuals or in associations so that the divine message of salvation becomes known and accepted by all persons throughout the world; this obligation has a greater impelling force in those circumstances in which people can hear the gospel and know Christ only through lay persons.

§2. Each lay person in accord with his or her condition is bound by a special duty to imbue and perfect the order of temporal affairs with the spirit of the gospel; they thus give witness to Christ in a special way in carrying out those affairs and in exercising secular duties.

Canon 241—§1. The diocesan bishop is to admit to the major seminary only those who are judged capable of dedicating themselves permanently to the sacred ministries in light of their human, moral, spiritual and intellectual characteristics, their physical and psychological health and their proper motivation.

§2. Before they are accepted, they must submit documents certifying that baptism and confirmation have been received and other documents which are required in accord with the prescriptions of the program for priestly formation.

§3. When persons seek admission after they have been dismissed from another seminary or from a religious institute, further testimony is required from their respective superior, especially regarding the cause of their dismissal or their leaving.

Canon 383—§1. In the exercise of his pastoral office a diocesan bishop is to show that he is concerned with all the Christian faithful who are committed to his care regardless of age, condition or nationality, both those who live within his territory and those who are staying in it temporarily; he is to extend his apostolic spirit to those who cannot sufficiently make use of ordinary pastoral care due to their condition in life and to those who no longer practice their religion.

§2. If he has faithful of a different rite within his diocese, he is to provide for their spiritual needs either by means of priests or parishes of that rite or by means of an episcopal vicar.

§3. He is to act with kindness and charity toward those who are not in full communion with the Catholic Church, fostering ecumenism as it is understood by the Church.

§4. He is to consider non-baptized as being committed to him in the Lord so that there may shine upon them the charity of Christ for whom the bishop must be a witness before all.

Canon 455—§1. The conference of bishops can issue general decrees only in those cases in which the common law prescribes it, or a special mandate of the Apostolic See, given either *motu proprio* or at the request of the conference, determines it.

§2. The general decrees mentioned in §1 can be validly passed in a plenary session only if two-thirds of the members of the conference having a deliberative vote approve them; such decrees do not have binding force, unless they have been legitimately promulgated, after having been reviewed by the Apostolic See.

§3. The manner of promulgation and the time from which the decrees take effect are to be determined by the conference of bishops itself.

§4. In the cases where neither the universal law nor a special mandate of the Apostolic See has granted the conference of bishops the power mentioned above in §1, the competence of individual diocesan bishops remains intact; and neither the conference nor its president may act in the name of all the bishops unless each and every bishop has given his consent.

Canon 519—The pastor is the proper shepherd of the parish entrusted to him, exercising pastoral care in the community entrusted to him under the authority of the diocesan bishop in whose ministry of Christ he has been called to share; in accord with the norm of law he carries out for his community the duties of teaching, sanctifying and governing, with the cooperation of other presbyters or deacons and the assistance of lay members of the Christian faithful.

Canon 528—§1. The pastor is obliged to see to it that the word of God in its entirety is announced to those living in the parish; for this reason he is to see to it that the lay Christian faithful are instructed in the truths of the faith, especially through the homily which is to be given on Sundays and holy days of obligation and through the catechetical formation which he is to give; he is to foster works by which the spirit of the gospel, including issues involving social justice, is promoted; he is to take special care for the Catholic education of children and of young adults; he is to make every effort with the aid of the Christian faithful, to bring the gospel message also to those who have ceased practicing their religion or who do not profess the true faith.

§2. The pastor is to see to it that the Most Holy Eucharist is the center of the parish assembly of the faithful; he is to work to see to it that the Christian faithful are nourished through a devout celebration of the sacraments and especially that they frequently approach the sacrament of the Most Holy Eucharist and the sacrament of penance; he is likewise to endeavor that they are brought to the practice of family prayer as well as to knowing and active participation in the sacred liturgy, which the pastor must supervise in his parish under the authority of the diocesan bishop, being vigilant lest any abuses creep in.

Canon 529—§1. In order to fulfill his office in earnest the pastor should strive to come to know the faithful who have been entrusted to his care; therefore he is to visit families, sharing the cares, worries, and especially the griefs of the faithful, strengthening them in the Lord, and correcting them prudently if they are wanting in certain areas; with a generous love he is to help the sick, particularly those close to death, refreshing them solicitously with the sacraments and commending their souls to God; he is to make a special effort to seek out the poor, the afflicted, the lonely, those exiled from their own land, and similarly those weighed down with special difficulties; he is also to labor diligently so that spouses and parents are supported in fulfilling their proper duties, and he is to foster growth in the Christian life within the family.

§2. The pastor is to acknowledge and promote the proper role which the lay members of the Christian faithful have in the Church's mission by fostering their associations for religious purposes; he is to cooperate with his own bishop and with the presbyterate of the diocese in working hard so that the faithful be concerned for parochial communion and that they realize that they are members both of the diocese and of the universal Church and participate in and support efforts to promote such communion.

Canon 530—The following functions are especially entrusted to the pastor:
    1° the administration of baptism;
    2° the administration of the sacrament of confirmation to those who are in danger of death, according to the norm of can. 883, 3°;
    3° the administration of Viaticum and the anointing of the sick with due regard for the prescription of can.

1003, §§2 and 3, as well as the imparting of the apostolic blessing;

4° the assistance at marriages and the imparting of the nuptial blessing;

5° the performing of funerals;

6° the blessing of the baptismal font during the Easter season, the leading of processions outside the church and the imparting of solemn blessings outside the church;

7° the more solemn celebration of the Eucharist on Sundays and holy days of obligation.

Canon 535—§1. Each parish is to possess a set of parish books including baptismal, marriage and death registers as well as other registers prescribed by the conference of bishops or the diocesan bishop; the pastor is to see to it that these registers are accurately inscribed and carefully preserved.

§2. In the baptismal register are also to be noted the person's confirmation and whatever affects the canonical status of the Christian faithful by reason of marriage, with due regard for the prescription of can. 1133, adoption, reception of sacred orders, perpetual profession in a religious institute, and change of rite; these notations are always to be noted on a document which certifies the reception of baptism.

§3. Each parish is to possess its own seal; documents which are issued to certify the canonical status of the Christian faithful as well as acts which can have juridic importance are to be signed by the pastor or his delegate and sealed with the parish seal.

§4. Each parish is to have a registry or archive in which the parish books are kept along with episcopal letters and other documents which ought to be preserved due to necessity or usefulness; all these are to be inspected by the diocesan bishop or his delegate during his visitation or at another suitable time; the pastor is to take care that they do not come into the hands of outsiders.

§5. The older parish books are also to be carefully preserved in accord with the prescriptions of particular law.

Canon 555—§1. In addition to the faculties legitimately granted him in particular law, a vicar forane has the duty and right:

1° to promote and coordinate the common pastoral activity within the vicariate;

2° to see to it that the clerics of his district lead a life which is in harmony with their state of life and diligently perform their duties;

3° to see to it that religious functions are celebrated in accord with the prescriptions of the sacred liturgy, that the good appearance and condition of the churches and of sacred furnishings are carefully maintained especially in the celebration of the Eucharist and the custody of the Blessed Sacrament, that the parish books are correctly inscribed and duly cared for, that ecclesiastical goods are carefully administered, and finally that the rectory is maintained with proper care.

§2. Within the vicariate entrusted to him the vicar forane:

1° is to see to it that clerics, in accord with the prescriptions of particular law and at the times stated in such law, attend theological lectures, meetings or conferences in accord with the norm of can. 272, §2 [apparently should read 279, §2—translator's note]

2° is to take care that the presbyters of his district have ready access to spiritual helps and is to be particularly concerned about those priests who find themselves in rather difficult circumstances or who are beset with problems.

§3. The vicar forane is to take care that the pastors of his district whom he knows to be seriously ill do not lack spiritual and material aids, while seeing to it that the funerals of those who die are celebrated with dignity; he is likewise to make provision that when they are sick or dying, the books, documents, sacred furnishings or other things which belong to the Church are not lost or transported elsewhere.

§4. The vicar forane is obliged to visit the parishes of his district in accord with the regulations made by the diocesan bishop.

Canon 645—§1. Before they are admitted to the novitiate, candidates must show proof of baptism, confirmation and free status.

§2. If it is a question of admitting clerics or those who have been admitted to another institute of consecrated life, a society of apostolic life or a seminary, there is further required the testimony of the local ordinary or major superior of the institute or society or of the rector of the seminary respectively.

§3. Proper law can demand other testimonies about the requisite suitability of candidates and their freedom from impediments.

Canon 748—§1. All persons are bound to seek the truth in matters concerning God and God's Church; by divine law they are also obliged and have the right to embrace and to observe that truth which they have recognized.

§2. Persons cannot ever be forced by anyone to embrace the Catholic faith against their conscience.

Canon 756—§1. As regards the universal Church the duty of proclaiming the gospel has been especially entrusted to the Roman Pontiff and to the college of bishops.

§2. As regards the particular church entrusted to them the individual bishops exercise this responsibility since within it they are the moderators of the entire ministry of the word; sometimes, several bishops simultaneously fulfill this office jointly for various churches at once in accord with the norm of law.

Canon 759—In virtue of their baptism and confirmation lay members of the Christian faithful are witnesses to the gospel message by word and by example of a Christian life; they can also be called upon to cooperate with the bishop and presbyters in the exercise of the ministry of the word.

Canon 785—§1. Catechists are to be employed in carrying out missionary work; catechists are those lay members of the Christian faithful who have been duly instructed, who stand out by reason of their Christian manner of life, and who devote themselves to expounding the gospel teaching and organizing liturgical functions and works of charity under the supervision of a missionary.

§2. Catechists are to be educated in schools destined for this purpose or, where such schools are lacking, under the supervision of missionaries.

Canon 788—§1. After a period of pre-catechumenate has elapsed, persons who have manifested a willingness to embrace faith in Christ are to be admitted to the catechumenate in liturgical ceremonies and their names are to be registered in a book destined for this purpose.

§2. Through instruction and an apprenticeship in the Christian life catechumens are suitably to be initiated into the mystery of salvation and introduced to the life of faith, liturgy, charity of the people of God and the apostolate.

§3. It is the responsibility of the conference of bishops to issue statutes by which the catechumenate is regulated; these statutes are to determine what things are to be expected of catechumens and define what prerogatives are recognized as theirs.

Canon 789—Through a suitable instruction neophytes are to be formed to a more thorough understanding of the gospel truth and the baptismal duties to be fulfilled; they are to be imbued with a love of Christ and of His Church.

Canon 838—§1. The supervision of the sacred liturgy depends solely on the authority of the Church which resides in the Apostolic See and, in accord with the law, the diocesan bishop.

§2. It is for the Apostolic See to order the sacred liturgy of the universal Church, to publish the liturgical books, to review their translations in to the vernacular languages and to see that liturgical ordinances are faithfully observed everywhere.

§3. It pertains to the conferences of bishops to prepare translations of the liturgical books into the vernacular languages, with the appropriate adaptations within the limits defined in the liturgical books themselves, and to publish them with the prior review by the Holy See.

§4. It pertains to the diocesan bishop in the church entrusted to him, within the limits of his competence, to issue liturgical norms by which all are bound.

Canon 842—§1. One who has not received baptism cannot be validly admitted to the other sacraments.

§2. The sacraments of baptism, confirmation, and the Most Holy Eucharist are so interrelated that they are required for full Christian initiation.

Canon 843—§1. The sacred ministers can not refuse the sacraments to those who ask for them at appropriate times, are properly disposed and are not prohibited by law from receiving them.

§2. Pastors of souls and the rest of the Christian faithful, according to their ecclesial function, have the duty to see that those who seek the sacraments are prepared to receive them by the necessary evangelization and catechetical formation, taking into account the norms published by the competent authority.

Canon 844—§1. Catholic ministers may licitly administer the sacraments to Catholic members of the Christian faithful only and, likewise, the latter may licitly receive the sacraments only from Catholic ministers with due regard for §§2, 3, and 4 of this canon, and can. 861, §2.

§2. Whenever necessity requires or genuine spiritual advantage suggests, and provided that the danger of error or indifferentism is avoided, it is lawful for the faithful for whom it is physically or morally impossible to approach a Catholic minister, to receive the sacraments of penance, Eucharist, and anointing of the sick from non-Catholic ministers in whose churches these sacraments are valid.

§3. Catholic ministers may licitly administer the sacraments of penance, Eucharist and anointing of the sick to members of the oriental churches which do not have full communion with the Catholic Church, if they ask on their own for the sacraments and are properly disposed. This holds also for members of other churches, which in the judgment of the Apostolic See are in the same condition as the oriental churches as far as these sacraments are concerned.

§4. If the danger of death is present or other grave necessity, in the judgment of the diocesan bishop or the conference of bishops, Catholic ministers may licitly administer these sacraments to other Christians who do not have full communion with the Catholic Church, who cannot approach a minister of their own community and on their own ask for it, provided they manifest Catholic faith in these sacraments and are properly disposed.

§5. For the cases in §§2, 3, and 4, neither the diocesan bishop nor the conference of bishops is to enact general norms except after consultation with at least the local competent authority of the interested non-Catholic church or community.

Canon 845—§1. The sacraments of baptism, confirmation and orders cannot be repeated since they imprint a character.

§2. If, after diligent investigation, there is still a prudent doubt whether these sacraments mentioned in §1 have been truly or validly conferred, they are to be conditionally conferred.

Canon 846—§1. The liturgical books approved by the competent authority are to be faithfully observed in the celebration of the sacraments; therefore no one on personal authority may add, remove or change anything in them.

§2. The ministers are to celebrate the sacraments according to their own rite.

Canon 847—§1. In the administration of sacraments in which the sacred oils are to be used, the minister must use oils pressed from olives or from other plants that have been recently consecrated or blessed by the bishop, with due regard for the prescription of can. 999, n. 2; he is not to use old oils unless there is some necessity.

Canon 849—Baptism, the gate to the sacraments, necessary for salvation in fact or at least in intention, by which men and women are freed from their sins, are reborn as children of God and, configured to Christ by an indelible character, are incorporated in the Church, is validly conferred only by washing with true water together with the required form of words.

Canon 851—It is necessary that the celebration of baptism be properly prepared. Thus:
    1° an adult who intends to receive baptism is to be admitted to the catechumenate and, to the extent possible, be led through the several stages to sacramental initiation, in accord with the order of initiation adapted by the conference of bishops and the special norms published by it;
    2° the parents of an infant who is to be baptized and likewise those who are to undertake the office of sponsor are to be properly instructed in the meaning of this sacrament and the obligations which are attached to it; personally or through others the pastor is to see to it that the parents are properly formed by pastoral directions and by common prayer, gathering several families together and where possible visiting them.

Canon 852—§1. What is prescribed in the canons on the baptism of an adult is applicable to all who are no longer infants but have attained the use of reason.

§2. One who is not of sound mind (*non sui compos*) is equated with an infant so far as baptism is concerned.

Canon 854—Baptism is to be conferred either by immersion or by pouring, the prescriptions of the conference of bishops being observed.

Canon 855—Parents, sponsors and the pastor are to see that a name foreign to a Christian mentality is not given.

Canon 861—§1. The ordinary minister of baptism is a bishop, presbyter or deacon, with due regard for the prescription of can. 530, n.1.

§2. If the ordinary minister is absent or impeded, a catechist or other person deputed for this function by the local ordinary confers baptism licitly as does any person with the right intention in case of necessity; shepherds of souls, especially the pastor, are to be concerned that the faithful be instructed in the correct manner of baptizing.

Canon 863— The baptism of adults, at least those who have completed fourteen years of age is to be referred to the bishop so that it may be conferred by him, if he judges it expedient.

Canon 865—§1. To be baptized, it is required that an adult have manifested the will to receive baptism, be sufficiently instructed in the truths of faith and in Christian obligations and be tested in the Christian life by means of the catechumenate; the adult is also to be exhorted to have sorrow for personal sins.

§2. An adult in danger of death may be baptized if, having some knowledge of the principal truths of faith, the person has in any way manifested an intention of receiving baptism and promises to observe the commandments of the Christian religion.

Canon 869—§1. If there is a doubt whether one has been baptized or whether baptism was validly conferred and the doubt remains after serious investigation, baptism is to be conferred conditionally.

§2. Those baptized in a non-Catholic ecclesial community are not to be baptized conditionally unless, after an examination of the matter and the form of words used in the conferral of baptism and after a consideration of the intention of an adult baptized person and of the minister of the baptism, a serious reason for doubting the validity of the baptism is present.

§3. If the conferral or the validity of the baptism in the cases mentioned §§1 and 2 remains doubtful, baptism is not to be conferred until the doctrine of the sacrament of baptism is explained to the person, if an adult, and the reasons for the doubtful validity of the baptism have been explained to the adult recipient or, in the case of an infant, to the parents.

Canon 873—Only one male or one female sponsor or one of each sex it to be employed.

Canon 874—§1. To be admitted to the role of sponsor, a person must:
 1° be designated by the one to be baptized, by the parents or the one who takes their place or, in their absence, by the pastor or minister and is to have the qualifications and intention of performing this role;
 2° have completed the sixteenth year, unless a different age has been established by the diocesan bishop or it seems to the pastor or minister that an exception is to be made for a just cause;
 3° be a Catholic who has been confirmed and has already received the sacrament of the Most Holy Eucharist and leads a life in harmony with the faith and the role to be undertaken;
 4° not be bound by an canonical penalty legitimately imposed or declared;
 5° not be the father or the mother of the one to be baptized;

§2. A baptized person who belongs to a non-Catholic ecclesial community may not be admitted except as a witness to baptism and together with a Catholic sponsor.

Canon 876—If it is not prejudicial to anyone, to prove the conferral of baptism, the declaration of a single witness who is above suspicion suffices or the oath of the baptized person, if the baptism was received at an adult age.

Canon 877—§1. The pastor of the place where the baptism is celebrated must carefully and without delay record in the baptismal book the names of those baptized making mention of the minister, parents, sponsors, witnesses if any and the place and date of the conferred baptism, together with an indication of the date and place of birth.

§2. If it is a question of a child born of an unmarried mother, the name of the mother is to be inserted if there is public proof of her maternity or if she asks this willingly, either in writing or before two witnesses; likewise the name of the father is to be inserted if his paternity has been proved either by some public document or by his own declaration before the pastor and two witnesses; in other cases, the name of the one baptized is recorded without any indication of the name of the father or the parents.

§3. If it is a question of an adopted child, the names of the adopting parents are to be recorded, and also, at least if this is to be done in the civil records of the region, the names of the natural parents, in accord with §§1 and 2, with due regard for the prescriptions of the conference of bishops.

Canon 878—If baptism was administered neither by the pastor nor in his presence, the minister of baptism, whoever it is, must inform the pastor of the parish in which the baptism was administered, so that he may record it in accord with canon 877, §1.

Canon 879—The sacrament of confirmation impresses a character and by it the baptized, continuing on the path of Christian initiation, are enriched by the gift of the Holy Spirit and bound more perfectly to the Church; it strengthens them and obliges them more firmly to be witnesses to Christ by word and deed and to spread and defend the faith.

Canon 880—§1. The sacrament of confirmation is conferred through anointing with chrism on the forehead, which is done by the imposition of the hand, and through the words prescribed in the approved liturgical books.

§2. The chrism to be used in the sacrament of confirmation must be consecrated by a bishop, even if the sacrament is administered by a presbyter.

Canon 882—The ordinary minister of confirmation is the bishop; a presbyter who has the faculty by virtue of either the common law or a special concession of competent authority also confers this sacrament validly.

Canon 883—The following have the faculty of administering confirmation by the law itself:
   1° within the limits of their territory, those who are equivalent in law to the diocesan bishop;
   2° with regard to the person in question, the presbyter who by reason of office or mandate of the diocesan bishop baptizes one who is no longer an infant or one already baptized whom he admits into full communion of the Catholic Church;
   3° with regard to those in danger of death, the pastor or indeed any presbyter.

Canon 885—§1. The diocesan bishop is obliged to see that the sacrament of confirmation is conferred on his subjects who properly and reasonably request it.

§2. A presbyter who has this faculty must use it for those in whose favor the faculty was granted.

Canon 889—§1. All baptized persons who have not been confirmed and only they are capable of receiving confirmation.

§2. Outside the danger of death, to be licitly confirmed it is required, if the person has the use of reason, that one be suitably instructed, properly disposed and able to renew one's baptismal promises.

Canon 891—The sacrament of confirmation is to be conferred on the faithful at about the age of discretion unless the conference of bishops determines another age or there is danger of death or in the judgment of the minister a grave cause urges otherwise.

Canon 893—§1. To perform the role of sponsor, it is necessary that a person fulfill the conditions mentioned in can. 874.

§2. It is desirable that the one who undertook the role of sponsor at baptism be sponsor for confirmation.

Canon 895—The names of the confirmed with mention of the minister, the parents and the sponsors, the place and the date of conferral of confirmation are to be noted in the confirmation register in the diocesan curia, or, where the conference of bishops or the diocesan bishop has prescribed it, in a book kept in the parish archive; the pastor must advise the pastor of the place of baptism about the conferral of confirmation so that notation be made in the baptismal register, in accord with the norm of can. 535, §2.

Canon 896—If the pastor of the place were not present, the minister either personally or through another is to inform him of the confirmation as soon as possible.

Canon 916—A person who is conscious of grave sin is not to celebrate Mass or to receive the Body of the Lord without prior sacramental confession unless a grave reason is present and there is no opportunity of confessing; in this case the person is to be mindful of the obligation to make an act of perfect contrition, including the intention of confessing as soon as possible.

Canon 918—It is highly recommended that the faithful receive Holy Communion during the celebration of the Eucharist itself, but it should be administered outside Mass to those who request it for a just cause, the liturgical rites being observed.

Canon 960—Individual and integral confession and absolution constitute the only ordinary way by which the faithful person who is aware of serious sin is reconciled with God and with the Church; only physical or moral impossibility excuses the person from confession of this type, in which case reconciliation can take place in other ways.

Canon 989—After having attained the age of discretion, each of the faithful is bound by an obligation faithfully to confess serious sins at least once a year.

Canon 1033—One is licitly promoted to orders only if he has received the sacrament of confirmation.

Canon 1050—For one to be promoted to sacred orders the following documents are required:
    1° certification that the studies prescribed by can. 1032, have been duly completed;
    2° certification that the diaconate has been received if it is a question of those to be ordained to the presbyterate;
    3° certification that baptism and confirmation have been received and that the ministries mentioned in can. 1035 have been received if it is a question of those to be promoted to the diaconate; also, certification that the declaration mentioned in can. 1036 has been made; and, if the ordinand who is to be promoted to the permanent diaconate is married, certification of the marriage that was celebrated and of the wife's consent.

Canon 1055—§1. The matrimonial covenant, by which a man

and a woman establish between themselves a partnership of the whole life, is by its nature ordered toward the good of the spouses and the procreation and education of offspring; this covenant between baptized persons has been raised by Christ the Lord to the dignity of a sacrament.

§2. For this reason a matrimonial contract cannot validly exist between persons unless it is also a sacrament by that fact.

Canon 1057—§1. Marriage is brought about through the consent of the parties, legitimately manifested between persons who are capable according to the law of giving consent; no human power can replace this consent.

§2. Matrimonial consent is an act of the will by which a man and a woman, through an irrevocable covenant, mutually give and accept each other in order to establish marriage.

Canon 1060—Marriage enjoys the favor of the law; consequently, when a doubt exists the validity of a marriage is to be upheld until the contrary is proven.

Canon 1061—§1. A valid marriage between baptized persons is called ratified only if it has not been consummated; it is called ratified and consummated if the parties have performed between themselves in a human manner the conjugal act which is per se suitable for the generation of children, to which marriage is ordered by its very nature and by which the spouses become one flesh.

§2. After marriage has been celebrated, if the spouses have cohabited consummation is presumed until the contrary is proven.

§3. An invalid marriage is called putative if it has been celebrated in good faith by at least one of the parties, until both parties become certain of its nullity.

Canon 1065—§1. If they can do so without serious inconvenience, Catholics who have not yet received the sacrament of confirmation are to receive it before being admitted to marriage.

§2. It is strongly recommended that those to be married approach the sacraments of penance and the Most Holy Eucharist so that they may fruitfully receive the sacrament of marriage.

Canon 1068—Unless contrary indications are present, in danger of death, if other means of proof cannot be obtained, it is sufficient that the parties affirm—even under oath, if the case warrants it—that they have been baptized and that they are not held back by any impediment.

Canon 1083—§1. A man before he has completed his sixteenth year of age, and likewise a woman before she has completed her fourteenth year of age, cannot enter a valid marriage.

§2. It is within the power of the conference of bishops to establish an older age for the licit celebration of marriage.

Canon 1085—§1. A person who is held to the bond of a prior marriage, even if it has not been consummated, invalidly attempts marriage.

§2. Even if a prior marriage is invalid or dissolved for any reason whatsoever, it is not on that account permitted to contract another before the nullity or the dissolution of the prior marriage has been legitimately and certainly established.

Canon 1086—§1. Marriage between two persons, one of whom is baptized in the Catholic Church or has been received into it and has not left it by means of a formal act, and the other of whom is non-baptized, is invalid.

§2. This impediment is not to be dispensed unless the conditions mention in cann. 1125 and 1126 are fulfilled.

§3. If at the time the marriage was contracted one party was commonly considered to be baptized or the person's baptism was doubted, the validity of the marriage is to be presumed in accord with the norm of can. 1060 until it is proven with certainty that one party was baptized and the other was not.

Canon 1107—Even if a marriage was entered invalidly by reason of an impediment or lack of form, the consent which was furnished is presumed to continue until its revocation has been proved.

Canon 1108—§1. Only those marriages are valid which are contracted in the presence of the local ordinary or the pastor or a priest or deacon delegated by either of them, who assist, and in the presence of two witnesses, according to the rules expressed in the following canons, with due regard for the exceptions mentioned in cann, 144, 1112, §1, 1116 and 1127, §§2 and 3.

§2. The one assisting at a marriage is understood to be only that person who, present at the ceremony, asks for the contractants' manifestation of consent and receives it in the name of the Church.

Canon 1109—Unless they have been excommunicated, interdicted or suspended from office or declared such, whether by sentence or decree, within the confines of their territory, the local ordinary and the pastor in virtue of their office, validly assist at the marriages of their subjects as well as of non-subjects provided one of the contractants is of the Latin rite.

Canon 1110—In virtue of their office and within the limits of their jurisdiction an ordinary and a personal pastor validly assist only at marriages involving at least one of their subjects.

Canon 1117—With due regard for the prescriptions of can. 1127, §2, the form stated above is to be observed whenever at least one of the contractants was baptized in the Catholic Church or was received into it and has not left it by a formal act.

Canon 1124—Without the express permission of the competent authority, marriage is forbidden between two baptized persons, one of whom was baptized in the Catholic Church or received into it after baptism and has not left it by a formal act, and the other of whom is a member of a church or ecclesial community which is not in full communion with the Catholic Church.

Canon 1125—The local ordinary can grant this permission if there is a just and reasonable cause; he is not to grant it unless the following conditions have been fulfilled:
1° the Catholic party declares that he or she is prepared to remove dangers of falling away from the faith and makes a sincere promise to do all in his or her power to have all the children baptized and brought up in the Catholic Church;
2° the other party is to be informed at an appropriate time of these promises which the Catholic party has to make, so that it is clear that the other party is truly aware of the promise and obligation of the Catholic party;
3° both parties are to be instructed on the essential ends and properties of marriage, which are not to be excluded by either party.

Canon 1137—Children conceived or born of a valid or putative marriage are legitimate.

Canon 1142— A non-consummated marriage between baptized persons or between a baptized party and a non-baptized party can be dissolved by the Roman Pontiff for a just cause, at the request of both parties or of one of the parties, even if the other party is unwilling.

Canon 1143—§1. A marriage entered by two non-baptized persons is dissolved by means of the pauline privilege in favor of the faith of a party who has received baptism by the very fact that a new marriage is contracted by the party who has been baptized, provided that the non-baptized party departs.

§2. The non-baptized party is considered to have departed if he or she does not wish to cohabit with the baptized party or does not wish to cohabit in peace without insult to the Creator unless, after receiving baptism, the baptized party gave the other party a just cause for departure.

Canon 1144—§1. In order for the baptized party to contract a new marriage validly, the non-baptized party must always be interrogated on the following points:

1° whether he or she also wishes to receive baptism;
2° whether he or she at least wishes to cohabit in peace with the baptized party without insult to the Creator.

§2. This interrogation must take place after baptism; for a serious reason, however, the local ordinary can permit this interrogation to take place before baptism, or even dispense for this interrogation either before or after the baptism, provided it is evident in light of at least a summary and extrajudicial process, that it cannot take place or that it would be useless.

Canon 1145—§1. As a rule, the interrogation is to take place on the authority of the local ordinary of the converted party; if the other spouse asks for a period of time during which to answer, the same ordinary is to grant it while warning the party that after this period has elapsed without any answer, the person's silence will be considered to be a negative answer.

§2. An interrogation carried out privately by the converted party is also valid and is indeed licit if the form prescribed above cannot be observed.

§3. In either case the fact that the interrogation took place and its outcome must legitimately be evident in the external forum.

Canon 1146—The baptized party has a right to contract a new marriage with a Catholic party:

1° if the other party answered negatively to the interrogation or if the interrogation has been legitimately omitted;

2° if the non-baptized party, interrogated or not, at first peacefully cohabited without insult to the Creator but afterwards departed without a just cause, with due regard for the prescriptions of cann. 1144 and 1145.

Canon 1147—For a serious cause the local ordinary can permit the baptized party who employs the pauline privilege to contract marriage with a non-Catholic party, whether baptized or not, while observing the prescriptions of the canons on mixed marriages.

Canon 1156—§1. To convalidate a marriage which is invalid due to a diriment impediment, it is required that the impediment cease or that it be dispensed and that at least the party who is aware of the impediment renew consent.

§2. This renewal of consent is required by ecclesiastical law for the validity of the convalidation even if both parties furnished consent at the beginning and have not revoked it later.

Canon 1158—§1. If the impediment is a public one, the consent is to be renewed by both parties according to the canonical form, with due regard for the prescription of can. 1127, §3.

§2. If the impediment cannot be proven to exist, it is sufficient that the consent be renewed privately and in secret by the party who is aware of the impediment, provided the other party perseveres in the consent already given, or by both parties when each of them knows about the impediment.

Canon 1168—The minister of the sacramentals is a cleric who has been given the necessary power; in accord with the norm of the liturgical books and according to the judgment of the local ordinary, some sacramentals can also be administered by lay persons who are endowed with the appropriate qualities.

Canon 1169—§1. Persons who possess the episcopal character as well as presbyters to whom it is permitted by law or by legitimate concession can validly perform consecrations and dedications.

§2. Any presbyter can impart blessings, except those which are reserved to the Roman Pontiff or to bishops.

§3. A deacon can impart only those blessings which are expressly permitted to him by law.

Canon 1170—Blessings, to be imparted especially to Catholics, can also be given to catechumens and even to non-Catholics unless a church prohibition precludes this.

Canon 1177—§1. As a rule the funeral rites for any of the faithful departed must be celebrated in his or her own parish church.

§2. However, any member of the Christian faithful or those commissioned to arrange for his or her funeral may choose another church for the funeral rites with the consent of its rector and after informing the departed person's pastor.

§3. If death has occurred outside the person's own parish, and the corpse has not been transferred to that parish and another church has not been legitimately chosen for the funeral, the funeral rites are to be celebrated in the church of the parish where the death occurred unless another church has been designated by particular law.

Canon 1183—§1. As regards funeral rites catechumens are to be considered members of the Christian faithful.

§2. The local ordinary can permit children to be given ecclesiastical funeral rites if their parents intended to baptize them but they died before their baptism.

§3. In the prudent judgment of the local ordinary, ecclesiastical funeral rites can be granted to baptized members of some non-Catholic church or ecclesial community unless it is evidently contrary to their will and provided their own minister is available.

Canon 1247—On Sundays and other holy days of obligation the faithful are bound to participate in the Mass; they are also to abstain from those labors and business concerns which impede the worship to be rendered to God, the joy which is proper to the Lord's Day, or the proper relaxation of mind and body.

Canon 1476—Anyone, whether baptized or not, can act in a trial; however, the respondent who has been legitimately cited must answer.

Canon 1674—The following are capable of challenging a marriage:
   1° the spouses;
   2° the promoter of justice when the nullity has become public, if the marriage cannot be convalidated or this is not expedient.

APPENDIX C

FACULTIES FOR ADULT INITIATION THAT MAY BE DELEGATED BY THE BISHOP

Certain powers connected with adult initiation and reception into the full communion of the Catholic church are reserved to the diocesan bishop. These powers may, however, be delegated by the bishop for the sake of competent and efficient administration and effective catechetical and liturgical life in the diocese. The faculties are in two categories: (A) those that the bishop may delegate to the head of the diocesan worship office and (B) those that he may delegate to pastors. The head of the diocesan worship office, whether cleric or lay, generally has an advanced degree in liturgy and/or is knowledgeable about the requirements of the Rite of Christian Initiation of Adults, and therefore is usually the person best qualified to handle the competencies listed under A.

A. FACULTIES THAT COULD BE DELEGATED BY THE DIOCESAN BISHOP TO THE HEAD OF THE DIOCESAN WORSHIP OFFICE:

1. to set up, regulate and promote the program of pastoral formation for catechumens (RCIA, 12; 34, §1; 77)

2. to depute catechists, truly worthy and properly prepared, to give the minor exorcisms and the blessings of the catechumens (RCIA, 12, 16, 34.5; 91, 96)

3. to decide whether and when, as circumstances warrant, the entire rite of Christian initiation may be celebrated outside the usual times (RCIA, 26; 34, §2)

4. to determine whether the additional rites listed in RCIA, 75, are to be incorporated (NCCB Statutes, 5; RCIA, 33, §5)

5. to permit the use of the abbreviated catechumenate in individual and exceptional cases as described in RCIA, 331–332, and the NCCB Statutes, 20 (RCIA, 34, §4)

6. to dispense, on the basis of some serious obstacle, from one scrutiny or, in extraordinary circumstances, even from two (RCIA, 34, §3; 331)

7. to decide in each case what rites are to be included or excluded in conferring conditional baptism (RCIA, 480)

B. FACULTIES THAT COULD BE GRANTED TO ALL PASTORS

1. to grant the mandate to celebrate adult initiation in the territory of the parish to a presbyter who lacks a pastoral office (NCCB Statutes, 12)

2. to entrust to a presbyter who lacks a pastoral office the celebration in the parish territory of the rite of reception of baptized Christians into the full communion of the Catholic church, which carries with it the faculty to confirm in accord with said rite (RCIA, 481; NCCB Statutes, 35)

3. in the territory of the parish to confirm uncatechized adult Catholics and to delegate this faculty to other presbyters (NCCB Statutes, 29)

APPENDIX D

INDEX OF CITATIONS FROM LITURGICAL BOOKS AND OTHER DOCUMENTS